Free Negro Owners of Slaves

in the

United States in 1830

Together with

Absentee Ownership of Slaves in the
United States in 1830

Compiled under the Direction of and edited by
CARTER G. WOODSON

NEGRO UNIVERSITIES PRESS

NEW YORK

Reprinted in 1968
by Negro Universities Press
A DIVISION OF GREENWOOD PUBLISHING CORP.
New York

Library of Congress Catalogue Card Number: 68-55923

Printed in the United States of America

FOREWORD

This statistical report on the free Negro ownership of slaves was made possible in 1921 when the Director of the Association for the Study of Negro Life and History obtained from the Laura Spelman Rockefeller Memorial an appropriation for the support of research into certain neglected aspects of Negro History. This special report, however, was not the objective of the Research Department of the Association. It developed rather as a by-product. In compiling statistics for the much larger report on *Free Negro Heads of Families in the United States in 1830,* the investigators found so many cases of Negroes owning slaves that it was decided to take special notice of this phase of the History of the free Negro.

The report on the *Absentee Ownership of Slaves in the United States in 1830* attached hereto developed in a similar way. The investigators were impressed also with the frequent occurrence of such wide separation of the master from the slave. In noting the cases of free Negro ownership it was a simple matter, then, to record also the cases of absentee ownership, and it was done accordingly.

CARTER G. WOODSON

WASHINGTON, D. C.,
April 1, 1924

INTRODUCTION

The aim of this report on the free Negro is to facilitate the further study of this neglected group. Most of these people have been forgotten, for persons supposedly well-informed in history are surprised to learn today that about a half million, almost one-seventh of the Negroes of this country, were free prior to the emancipation in 1865. It is hardly believed that a considerable number of Negroes were owners of slaves themselves, and in some cases controlled large plantations.

There were several reasons for selecting the census of 1830. In the first place, the earlier reports do not give as much information as the census of 1830. At that time, moreover, the free Negroes had about reached their highest mark as a distinct class. The reaction which set in earlier in the century restricted their freedom and in many cases expelled them from the South. This census, then, evidently reports the names of a larger number of representative free Negroes than any other census prior to their debasement to a lower status or their migration from the South. This trek reached its highest point between 1830 and 1835. Most of the free Negroes in the North in 1830, therefore, had been there for some years.

The census records show that the majority of the Negro owners of slaves were such from the point of view of philanthropy. In many instances the husband purchased the wife or vice versa. The slaves belonging to such families were few compared with the large numbers found among the whites on the well-developed plantations. Slaves of Negroes were in some cases the children of a free father who had purchased his wife. If he did not thereafter emancipate the mother, as so many such husbands failed to do, his own children were born his slaves and were thus reported by the enumerators.

v

Some of these husbands were not anxious to liberate their wives immediately. They considered it advisable to put them on probation for a few years, and if they did not find them satisfactory they would sell their wives as other slaveholders disposed of Negroes. For example, a Negro shoemaker in Charleston, South Carolina, purchased his wife for $700; but, on finding her hard to please, he sold her a few months thereafter for $750, gaining $50 by the transaction. The editor personally knew a man in Cumberland County, Virginia, whose mother was purchased by his father who had first bought himself. Becoming enamored of a man slave, she gave him her husband's manumission papers that they might escape together to free soil. Upon detecting this plot, the officers of the law received the impression that her husband had turned over the papers to the slave and arrested the freedman for the supposed offense. He had such difficulty in extricating himself from this complication that his attorney's fees amounted to $500. To pay them he disposed of his faithless wife for that amount.

Benevolent Negroes often purchased slaves to make their lot easier by granting them their freedom for a nominal sum, or by permitting them to work it out on liberal terms. John Barry Meachum, a Negro Baptist minister in St. Louis, thus came into possession of as many as twenty slaves by 1836. The exploitation type of Negro slaveholder, moreover, sometimes feeling the sting of conscience, liberated his slaves. Thus did Samuel Gibson, a Negro of Mississippi, in 1844, when he brought his six slaves to Cincinnati, Ohio, and settled them on free territory.

Having economic interests in common with the white slaveholders, the Negro owners of slaves often enjoyed the same social standing. It was not exceptional for them to attend the same church, to educate their children in the same private school, and to frequent the same places of amusement. Under such circumstances miscegenation easily followed. While those taking the census of 1830 did not generally record such facts, the few who did, as in the case of Nansemond County, Virginia, reported a situation which today would be considered alarming. In this particular County there appeared among the slaveholders free Negroes designated as Jacob of Read and white wife and Syphe of Matthews and white wife. Others reported with white wives were not slaveholders.

Practically all of these Negro slaveholders were in the South.[1] Slavery, however, at that time had not been ex-

[1] These facts were extracted from the manuscript schedules returned by those who took the census of the United States in 1830. After C. G. Woodson, the editor, had first copied the record of one state to acquaint himself in detail with the information given in these census reports, the statistics were then copied under his direction by three persons. One of them has had the advantage of two years' normal training after finishing high school, and two of them have completed college courses at Howard University and at the University of Michigan. The matter thus collected was then verified by Mr. Alrutheus A. Taylor, an alumnus of Michigan and a Harvard Master of Arts in History and Economics, now employed as Associate Investigator of the Association for the Study of Negro Life and History. Further verification was made by C. G. Woodson.

These records were copied just as those who took the census returned their findings. The only change made in the case of Negro Owners of slaves was to write the family name first, a rule which these enumerators did not all follow.

Some enumerators made no distinction as to race in recording the names, but merely indicated the status of the head of the family under free persons of color. Other enumerators wrote *Negro, Cold.* or *Colored,* or used *F. N.* for free Negro, *F. of C.* for free person of color, *F. M. C.* for free man of color, *F. W. C.* for free woman of color, or *fb.* and *fbk.* for free black, directly after the name.

The question mark after a name or a figure or in a column indicates that the record is such that the fact could not be accurately determined.

The column giving the AGE does not every time show the age of the head of the family. In some instances the age of the head of the family cannot be exactly figured out. The age here given is that of the oldest person in the family of the sex indicated as the head of the family. The record as to sex, moreover, is often confusing. The name of a male is sometimes given as the head of the family while the sex is indicated as female or vice versa. In eighty per cent of the cases which the investigator has tested, however, it can be shown that this is the actual age of the head of the family.

" 10–24 "-means 10 years of age and under 24, and " 24–36 " means 24 years of age and under 36. 100 means a hundred or more than a hundred years old.

The column entitled SLAVES gives the number of slaves owned by the head of the family.

TOTAL means the number of persons in the family together with all of

terminated altogether in the North, and even there the Negro was following in the footsteps of the white man, as this report will show.

In the South where almost all of the Negro slaveholders were, moreover, we find some of them competing with the large planters in the number of slaves they owned. Most of such Negro proprietors lived in Louisiana, South Carolina, Maryland and Virginia, as did the majority of all such slave owners. There are, moreover, a few instances of confusing absentee ownership with Negro ownership. Sometimes a free Negro had charge of a plantation, but did not own the slaves himself, and the enumerator returned him as the owner.

Excepting those of Louisiana, one may say that most of the Negro owners of slaves lived in urban communities. In those parts of the South where the influence of the kind planter near the coast was not felt, the Negro owner of slaves did not frequently appear. The free Negroes themselves, moreover, encountered such difficulties in the lower South and Southwest that they had to seek more hospitable communities in free States.

By 1840 the trend toward degrading the free Negro to a lower status had become evident even in the apparently benevolent slaveholding States. Just before the outbreak of the Civil War the free Negro was receiving practically no consideration in the South and very little in the North. History here repeats itself, then, in showing the varying attitude of the whites toward the blacks in the cycles of national development.

the slaves. This enables the student to figure out for himself whether the slaveholding was an act of exploitation or of benevolence. The small number of slaves, however, does not always signify benevolence on the part of the owner.

ALABAMA

Name	Slaves	Total	Age	Name	Slaves	Total	Age
CLARKE COUNTY				Chastang, Basil	1	10	55–100
Meggs, James	1	2	36–55	Chastang, Bastiste	1	3	36–55
Harris, P. T.	24	25	55–100	Chastang, Zane	1	3	55–100
Hatcher, William	2	3	36–55	Chastang, Zeno	5	15	36–55
Stapleton, Joseph	1	2	36–55	Chastang, Louisa	14	19	55–100
Monack, David	27	28	55–100	Nicholas, Jasma	3	5	24–36
				City of Mobile			
DALLAS COUNTY				Rutgeron, Frances	1	2	24–36
Smith, Tom	4	14	36–55	Ferer, Clara	4	6	24–36
				Laurendine, Benjamin	1	7	24–36
LAWRENCE COUNTY				Rozieste, Burnadoz	14	32	24–36
Royall, Lewis	1	3	55–100	Guile, Mad. O.	4	10	55–100
				Chastang, Frances	1	7	55–100
MADISON COUNTY				Gregg, Frances	2	8	24–36
First and Second Ranges of Townships				Mary, Mad.	6	8	36–55
Davis, Betsey	1	7	36–55	Rozieste, Peir	6	14	24–36
Stewart, James F.	2	3	36–55	Boshong, Madam	16	23	36–55
				MONROE COUNTY			
Third and Fourth Ranges of Townships				Sizemore (?), Arthur	3	8	55–100
Robinson, John	4	7	24–36	Sizemore (?), Susanna	2	7	36–55
Blanks, Paschal	2	4	24–36				
Hunt, Lewis	1	4	24–36	**MONTGOMERY COUNTY**			
Hunster, Nancy	1	8	36–55	Fowler (de), Oxey	1	3	55–100
Findley, Jenny	1	2	24–36	Lanton Joseph (F. of C.)	2	11	55–100
Evans, John	1	3	36–55				
Winn, Andrew	2	3	55–100	**PERRY COUNTY**			
				Thomas, Frederick V.	1	8	55–100
MOBILE COUNTY							
Minnie	1	6	36–55	**SHELBY COUNTY**			
Key, Lawrence	4	11	24–36	Hadsen, Isah	1	12	36–55
Chastang, Theresa	2	3	100–				
Simore, Felix	1	10	55–100	**WASHINGTON COUNTY**			
Colderen, Simore	3	8	24–36	Saunsha, John	2	3	36–55
Andre, Sylvester	2	10	36–55				
Andre, Mademitian	6	15	36–55	**WILCOX COUNTY**			
Simore, Jane	10	13	36–55	Martin, John	1	3	36–55

ARKANSAS TERRITORY

Name	Slaves	Total	Age				
LAFAYETTE COUNTY							
Free Bob	3	4	36–55				

CONNECTICUT

Name	Slaves	Total	Age				
FAIRFIELD COUNTY							
Demosat, Amos	1	6	55–100				

DELAWARE

Name	Slaves	Total	Age	Name	Slaves	Total	Age
NEWCASTLE COUNTY				Delahow, Jacob	1	6	36–55
Davis, Samuel B.	3	4	10–24				
Millis, Charles	1	3	24–36	**SUSSEX COUNTY**			
Porter, Jessee	5	10	24–36	Mosley, Peter	6	7	100–
Dale, Hannah	1	2	36–55	Sirmon, Caleb	1	8	36–55
Tibut, Daniel	2	3	36–55	Richards, Robert	1	3	36–55

1

DISTRICT OF COLUMBIA

Name	Slaves	Total	Age	Name	Slaves	Total	Age
Washington				Netter, Sarah..........	2	3	24–36
Fourth Ward				Matthews, Luke........	1	2	36–55
Colored, Robinson......	3	3	36–55	Baltimore, James......	1	2	24–36
" Clark........	1	7	24–36	Sewell, Rd..........	1	5	36–55
" Hanson, H....	6	7	24–36	Gordon, Wm..........	2	5	10–24
" Joice......	4	4	24–36	Proctor, Os..........	1	7	36–55
" Johnson......	4	4	36–55	Glasgow, John..........	1	3	55–100
" Brown........	4	5	24–36	Brooke, Bétsy..........	1	2	55–100
" Dubbon......	9	9	36–55	Jenifer, Mary..........	1	9	36–55
" Tillman......	5	5	24–36	Shaw, Simon..........	6	8	36–55
Bell..........	1	4	55–100	Curtis, Samuel..........	6	7	10–24
Dyson..........	1	6	24–36	Gant, Catharine........	3	4	55–100
Colored, Jones, J......	1	3	36–55	Fowler, Mary..........	1	5	24–36
" Sims, Benj......	3	4	36–55	Eglin, Harry..........	6	8	24–36
" Brooks, P.....	1	6	55–100	Moore, John..........	2	5	10–24
" Allison, Wm. :..	1	2	36–55	Ambush, Edward.......	1	6	36–55
" Hicks, Sandy...	1	3	36–55	Bowman, Eliza..........	1	5	36–55
" McKenzie, J....	1	2	10–24	Lowry, Scilla..........	1	2	55–100
Simpson, E..........	2	7	24–36	Doyne, Benedict........	1	6	24–36
Jackson..........	1	3	10–24	Henderson, Godfrey.....	2	3	10–24
Reed, J..........	1	3	24–36	Myers, Charles..........	1	2	24–36
Adams, W..........	1	7	24–36	Edwards, Griffin..........	1	2	10–24
Thompson, J..........	3	9	36–55	Shorter, Luke..........	1	4	24–36
Colored, Bonnell, Benj...	1	5	24–36	Bowen, Nancy..........	1	2	36–55
" Campbell, Wm.	1	2	36–55	Digs, Frank..........	2	4	10–24
" Allen, N........	1	7	36–55	Diggs, Anthony........	1	9	24–36
" Dyer, H........	2	4	36–55	Peters, Nancy..........	1	5	36–55
" West, P........	1	2	10–24	Patterson, Robert......	1	7	36–55
" Leatherberry, L.	1	5	24–36				
" Smiler, M......	1	5	36–55	WASHINGTON COUNTY			
" Butter, J.......	1	2	36–55	*East of Rock Creek and*			
" Mann, Ths....	1	2	55–100	*West of 7th Street*			
" Simms, A.......	1	4	24–36	*Turnpike*			
Bowen, H..........	4	6	24–36	Brooke, Robert..........	1	9	36–55
Jackson, A..........	6	8	55–100	Coats, Nancy..........	1	2	55–100
Colored, Jenkins, F.....	1	2	10–24				
Dexter, S..........	1	2	55–100	*Georgetown*			
Colored, Cooper, J.......	1	5	24–36	Moore, Mordecai.......	2	3	36–55
" Brown........	4	5	55–100	Murphy, Nathan.......	2	3	36–55
" Rivers........	1	4	36–55	Hawkins, Walter........	5	8	36–55
" Liverpool......	4	5	36–55	Cole, Horace..........	1	6	36–55
Gates..........	1	7	24–36	Brown, David..........	1	5	24–36
Turner..........	1	4	55–100	Tolson, Francis..........	1	7	36–55
Hatton, Ricd..........	1	2	36–55	Wilson, Jeffry..........	1	5	36–55
Neale, S..........	3	4	10–24	Freeman, Ignatius......	1	2	55–100
Manning, Amelia......	5	6	10–24	Dyson, Jno..........	1	4	24–36
Sims, Richard..........	1	3	24–36	Smith, Elizh..........	1	3	24–36
Blue, Samuel..........	4	5	36–55	Bivens, Richd..........	1	7	55–100
Smith, John..........	1	5	24–36	Chew, Saml. (principal) .	8	16	24–36
Neale, Kitty..........	1	3	24–36	Johnson, Fredk..........	1	5	24–36
Ashley, Martha..........	4	7	36–55	Littemon, Richd........	2	3	55–100
Dorsey, Kitty..........	2	6	24–36	Eglan, Saml..........	1	2	55–100
Norris, Kitty..........	1	5	36–55	Chapman, Benjn........	1	2	55–100
Grant, Titus..........	1	3	36–55	Key, Ann..........	2	5	24–36
Lewis, James..........	1	4	24–36	Williams, Susan..........	1	6	55–100
Mann, Eliza..........	1	2	24–36	Allen, Nathan..........	2	3	10–24
Chambers, Ellen........	2	4	55–100	Woodward, Lamber.....	1	5	10–24

DISTRICT OF COLUMBIA—*Continued*

Name	Slaves	Total	Age	Name	Slaves	Total	Age
Georgetown—Cont.				Coffee, Nicholas	1	3	36–55
Chase, Resin	1	3	36–55	Tarey, Andw	1	3	55–100
Washington, Geo. C.	1	6	10–24				
Mason, Josh	4	6	36–55	ALEXANDRIA COUNTY			
Lancaster, Conky	1	3	55–100	Lawrence, John	3	5	24–36
Butler, Ann	3	4	36–55	Kur & Fitzhugh	1	6	24–36
Washington. Walter	1	2	55–100	Brown, Henry	1	11	36–55
Brown, Isaac	1	6	24–36	Hepburn, Moses	2	5	10–24
Sims, Samuel	1	2	36–55	Myers, Abraham	1	7	36–55
Dines, Peter	1	2	36–55	Bend, Coffie	1	2	36–55
Coffee, Catharin	3	4	24–36	Merrise, Mima	1	2	24–36
Travers, Josh	1	2	24–36	Brown, Grace	1	2	55–100
Lee, Danl	1	3	55–100	Addison, Mary	1	2	36–55
Fenwick, Wm	1	3	10–24	Townsend, James	1	9	36–55
Boswell, Anthy	1	3	55–100	Chinn, Carlus	1	5	24–36
Downes, Susanna	1	7	55–100				

FLORIDA

Name	Slaves	Total	Age	Name	Slaves	Total	Age
ESCAMBIA COUNTY				ST. JOHNS COUNTY			
Fio (or Tio), Joseph M.	3	11	24–36	*St. Augustine*			
Bara, Doretea	3	9	24–36	Pepino, Mary	1	8	55–100
Muertre, Ann	6	11	55–100	Pepino, Valentine	3	8	55–100
Sachet, Gabriel Bertram	1	10	36–55	Clarke, James	3	9	24–36
Hinard, Eufroinne	12	14	55–100	Fish, Clarisa	1	10	36–55
Rouby, Joseph	6	10	36–55	Williams, Sampson	7	11	36–55
Coca, Carmelite	1	5	24–36	Perpall, Gabriel	39	40	55–100
				Sanches, Susan	4	5	36–55
NASSAU COUNTY							
Kingsley, Sophy	2	4	24–36				

GEORGIA

Name	Slaves	Total	Age	Name	Slaves	Total	Age
BURKE COUNTY				Crivillier, Hager	3	6	36–55
Nunes, Charles (colored)	2	6	36–55	Thompson, C.	2	3	10–24
Nunes, Joseph (colored)	6	7	24–36	Craig, Ann	3	12	55–100
Nunes, Janet (colored)	3	6	24–36	Merrillie, Jane	2	3	36–55
				Cruvillier, Justine	6	11	36–55
CAMDEN COUNTY				Jackson, Ragis	2	10	24–36
Brewer, Betsey	1	6	24–36	Gibbons, John	1	4	24–36
				Brown, Rebecca	2	6	24–36
CARROLL COUNTY				Malligo, William	3	6	36–55
Rowe, Arch	9	16	24–36	Whitfield, Sampson	1	5	24–36
Petit, Thomas	7	9	36–55	Harris, F.	1	4	36–55
Cornsilk	3	8	55–100	Luvett, Catherine	1	7	36–55
				Giblory, John	8	12	36–55
CHATHAM COUNTY				Darling, Massa	2	4	36–55
City of Savannah				Grant, Jane	1	2	36–55
Galineau, Rose	1	3	55–100	Wilson, William	3	6	36–55
Cunningham, Harry	7	9	55–100	Greenfield, Allen	6	8	24–36
Woodhouse, Robert	2	7	24–36	Ross, Cudjoe	5	8	36–55
Tenack, Mary	4	14	55–100	Netherclift, Dick	3	4	36–55
Tabeau, Manet	1	9	36–55				
Shomaca, Louisa	1	3	10–24	ELBERT COUNTY			
Ragis, Poline	2	7	36–55	Harper, Grace	1	17	36–55
Teice, M.	2	3	55–100				
Jackson, Susan	6	12	100–	EMANUEL COUNTY			
Neusome, Polly	3	6	36–55	Ruis (Lewis) (?), Polly	1	3	10–24

GEORGIA—*Continued*

Name	Slaves	Total	Age	Name	Slaves	Total	Age
FAYETTE COUNTY				Bush, Maria	2	4	10–24
Turner, James	2	13	36–55	Cobb, Billy	1	4	36–55
Turner, Silas	1	7	24–36	Monroe, Maria	1	7	24–36
Turner, Moses T	1	10	36–55	Haynes, John	3	4	36–55
				Hicks, Betsey	4	12	55–100
GREENE COUNTY				Brown, Josiah	7	8	24–36
Perry, Betsey	25	26	55–100	Dent, Fred and Jacob	6	12	36–55
				Carns, Lucy	1	8	36–55
MUSCOGEE COUNTY				Smith, Turner	6	15	24–36
Guardian, Phelps	2	3	55–100	Hill, Phillis	4	5	55–100
RANDOLPH COUNTY				**SCREVEN COUNTY**			
Triplett, Jim	2	5	55–100	Nicholson, Thomas	7	8	36–55
Dobbins, Amy	4	8	55–100				
Brown, Milly	3	7	36–55	**WARREN COUNTY**			
				Steth, Dan'l, of Col	1	6	36–55
RICHMOND COUNTY							
City of Augusta				**WILKES COUNTY**			
Moore, Isabella	4	6	24–36	Hoxey, William	1	7	36–55
Kelly, Betsey	2	6	24–36				

ILLINOIS

Name	Slaves	Total	Age	Name	Slaves	Total	Age
UNION COUNTY				**PEORIA AND PUTNAM**			
Robinson, Robert	1	3	55–100	**COUNTIES AND**			
				TERRITORY			
HAMILTON COUNTY				**ATTACHED**			
Shawnee Town				Croaker, Francis	1	4	24–36
Hubbard, Benjamin	3	7	36–55				
Equality Township				**RANDOLPH COUNTY**			
Cheek, Isham	1	12	36–55	Louvier, Margaret	2	5	55–100
Henderson, Louisa	2	6	24–36				
Clark, Gracey	1	7	55–100				

KENTUCKY

Name	Slaves	Total	Age	Name	Slaves	Total	Age
ADAIR COUNTY				**CHRISTIAN COUNTY**			
Burbridge, Sawney	2	2	36–55	*Hopkinsville*			
				Cocke, Michael	3	4	36–55
BARREN COUNTY				**CLARKE COUNTY**			
Force, Leander	1	3	55–100	Dudley, John	1	2	55–100
BOURBON COUNTY				Birth, George	1	3	36–55
Allen, Peter	2	4	55–100	**FAYETTE COUNTY**			
Wallace. Sally	1	2	36–55	*Lexington*			
Jones, Isaac	1	2	55–100	Scott, Nancy, Col'd			
Monday, James	1	3	36–55	woman	2	3	10–24
Grant, Peter	1	5	36–55	Whiting, Peter, Col'd			
Gabriel	1	3	36–55	man	1	2	24–36
Heathman, Allen	3	4	24–36	Gray, Rob't, Col'd man	4	6	24–36
Hurley, Edmon	1	5	55–100	Lewis, Charlotte, Col'd	1	3	55–100
Brooks, Stephen	2	4	36–55	Bird, Rich'd, Col'd man	1	2	36–55
BRACKEN COUNTY				Tucker, Wm., Col'd man	1	6	24–36
Thomas, Lethia	1	3	36–55	Smith, Jesse, Col'd man	1	2	36–55
BULLITT COUNTY				Keifer, Nathan, Col'd			
Mt. Washington				man	4	6	24–36
Ellison, Isaac	3	5	36–55	Tibbs, Benj'n	1	5	100–
Oldridge, Bash	1	3	55–100	Brittain, Jane	4	8	24–36

KENTUCKY—*Continued*

Name	Slaves	Total	Age	Name	Slaves	Total	Age
Lexington—Cont.				*City of Louisville*			
Travis, Hannah, Col'd woman	2	4	55–100	Cozzens, Betty	1	2	36–55
Brakenridge, Wittshire, Col'd woman	3	5	36–55	Straws, David	2	4	24–36
Phillips, Harvey	1	2	36–55?	Merriwether, Frank	3	6	36–55
Lee, Frank, and Nich's Black, Col'd men	3	5	55–100	Brigadier, Dan'l	1	2	36–55
				Sally (a Free woman)	1	2	36–55
FAYETTE COUNTY				JESSAMINE COUNTY			
Davis, Peter	2	7	55–100	Higenbothan, Judith	1	8	36–55
Martin, Adam B.	1	3	55–100	Anthony of colour	3	5	55–100
Howard, Isaac	2	3	55–100	William a man of color	3	4	36–55
Burk, William	1	4	55–100				
Caulden, Benjamin	4	5	36–55	KNOX COUNTY			
Francess, Peter	7	8	24–36	Goins, Isaiah	7	8	36–55
Williams, Ben	1	3	55–100				
Shores, Anaka	1	6	36–55	LOGAN COUNTY			
Allen, Jer'y	9	10	36–55	*Russellville*			
Allen, Alex'dr	2	4	55–100	Valentine, Nicholas	2	5	24–36
Dunlap, Samuel	1	2	36–55	Buckner, Robert	4	5	55–100
Clark, Rhody	1	10	36–55	Jones, Edward	1	5	24–36
Smith, Robt.	6	7	55–100	Husketh, Isham	3	16	36–55
				Barber, William	4	5	36–55
FLEMING COUNTY							
Eastern Division				MADISON COUNTY			
Truett, Jacob (A colored man)	3	5	36–55	White, George	4	6	55–100
				MASON COUNTY			
FRANKLIN COUNTY				Bowles, Thomas F.	1	9	24–36
North Division				Glasford, John	1	3	36–55
Frankfort				Cooper, Edward	1	5	24–36
Mordecai, Harry	4	12	36–55	Markham, H.	1	6	36–55
Jones, David	2	4	55–100	Wann, Roseann	3	4	36–55
Ward, John	1	3	36–55	More, Charles	6	8	36–55
Chiles, Burrel	2	4	55–100	Baylor, Ann	1	7	55–100
Goin, John S.	1	12	36–55	Toliver, Edmond	1	4	36–55
Brown, Samuel	1	4	36–55	Diggs, Acam	6	7	36–55
				Washington			
GRAVES COUNTY				*West of Main Street*			
Keeling, Alias	3	7	24–36	Miles, Peggy	1	2	55–100
				Lightfoot, John	1	3	55–100
GREENE COUNTY				Johnson, Isaac	1	3	36–55
Malone, Thos.	4	5	36–55	MERCER COUNTY			
				Harrodsburg			
HARRISON COUNTY				Harris, Anderson	2	8	36–55
West Side of Licking River				Harris, Ben	2	4	36–55
Berton, Benjamin	3	5	36–55	Easton, Spencer	4	5	24–36
				Melvin, Fielding	2	4	24–36
HENDERSON COUNTY				Fry, Jemima	1	5	24–36
Pointer, Liverpool	4	5	36–55	Jenkins, Hercules	1	4	55–100
				Warman, George	1	3	55–100
				Beaty, Adam	1	5	24–36
JEFFERSON COUNTY				Robinson, Sanko	2	6	55–100
Gray, J. T.	4	5	24–36	MONTGOMERY COUNTY			
				Lee, Richard	2	3	55–100

KENTUCKY—*Continued*

Name	Slaves	Total	Age	Name	Slaves	Total	Age
NELSON COUNTY				*North of the Road from*			
Bardstown				*Frankfort to Louisville*			
Smiley, Thomas........	3	4	55–100	Henson, Jim...........	2	3	36–55
Cocke, Joe............	1	4	36–55				
Rudd, Thomas........	2	3	36–55	WARREN COUNTY			
Aud, George...........	5	6	24–36	*Bowling Green*			
				Palmore, Jane..........	2	8	24–36
NICHOLAS COUNTY				Russell, Bazzle.........	2	3	36–55
Mallery, George.......	1	3	36–55				
				WASHINGTON COUNTY			
ROCKCASTLE COUNTY				*South of Main Street,*			
Cable, David..........	1	3	36–55	*Springfield*			
				Palmer, Robert C.......	2	3	100–
SHELBY COUNTY				Sandy, Ignatius.........	2	4	36–55
South of the Main road							
from Shelbyville to Louis-				WOODFORD COUNTY			
ville and from the Bridge				Miller, Joe.............	1	3	36–55
on Clear Creek to the Mt.				Corbin, Lawrence.......	1	4	55–100
Eden road thence with Sd.				Tutt, Betty............	7	8	55–100
road to Gayaways and				Campbell, Billy.........	8	10	55–100
down the Bardstown road				Mason, Henry..........	2	3	55–100
to the spencer line				Stratford, Tom.........	2	5	55–100
Edwards, John.........	1	3	36–55	Hardy, Ambrose........	1	3	55–100
				Harvey, Richard........	2	5	36–55
Shelbyville				Cloak, Samuel..........	3	4	36–55
North Main Street				Twiner, Nathan........	4	6	24–36
Short, Peter...........	1	3	36–55	Hawkins, Joel..........	3	8	55–100
				Weaver, Moses.........	1	8	36–55
North of Road from Louis-				Ritchie, Jordan.........	1	4	36–55
ville to Frankfort							
Harris, Hannah........	3	4	55–100				

LOUISIANA

Name	Slaves	Total	Age	Name	Slaves	Total	Age
ASCENSION PARISH				BATON ROUGE			
Jacques...............	4	8	100–	Benjamin..............	4	8	10–24
Talmaire, Pommela.....	4	6	10–24	Tomatiste, Alexandre....	1	2	24–36
Trauppe, Jean..........	1	7	55–100	Lange, Joseph..........	5	18	36–55
Quezer, François........	1	8	36–55				
Grace, Dominique.......	1	2	24–36	IBERVILLE			
				Lacour, Antoine........	18	26	55–100
ASSUMPTION				Bory, Augustin.........	20	26	36–55
Françoise, Mademoiselle.	3	4	24–36	De Landre, Georges.....	46	56	36–55
Julienne, Miss François..	2	8	100–	Honoré, Widow Zacharie.	21	29	36–55
Poche, Joseph..........	3	8	36–55	Dubuclet, Madame An-			
François, Jacques.......	4	6	36–55	toine................	44	52	55–100
				Riccard, Madame Ciprien	35	46	36–55
AVOYELLES							
Barzanna, Julien........	1	8	36–55	JEFFERSON			
				Veraunt, L., f.m.c......	4	10	24–36
CATAHOULA				Martin, J. W., f.w.c.....	4	10	55–100
Bowie, James (F.M.C.)..	3	11	36–55	Foltz, J. P., f.m.c........	5	9	24–36
				Pierre, M. J., f.w.c......	3	7	24–36
CONCORDIA				Langles, P., f.w.c........	10	19	55–100
Victor, Madam.........	6	9	36–55	Bowler, J. B., f.m.c......	6	11	36–55
				Augustin, J., f.m.c......	6	18	55–100
EAST BATON ROUGE				Sandors, M., f.m.c......	1	10	55–100
Marianne.............	1	9	36–55	Dauphin, M. T., f.w.c. ..	10	25	55–100
Delande, M. Joseph.....	4	10	36–55	Bakis, H. (?), f.m.c.....	1	8	55–100
Boyd, Robert..........	7	12	36–55				

LOUISIANA—*Continued*

Name	Slaves	Total	Age	Name	Slaves	Total	Age
JEFFERSON—*Cont.*				PLAQUEMINES			
Drespie, L., f.m.c........	1	3	55–100	Castourling, Jean........	3	10	55–100
Rosare, M., f.m.c........	1	9	36–55	Molly.................	6	10	24–36
Lavand, M., f.m.c.......	5	8	55–100	Duplessis, Valery.......	17	24	36–55
Max, M., f.m.c..........	1	3	55–100	Duplessis, Cazimer......	3	6	24–36
Brim, C., f.m.c..........	1	3	36–55	Duplessis, Honore.......	4	6	36–55
Rime, F., f.m.c.........	4	6	24–36	Duplessis, Michel.......	5	6	36–55
Dauphin, O., f.m.c......	4	8	24–36	Duplessis, Ciprien......	6	9	36–55
Sanlet, T., f.m.c........	12	20	55–100	Troupar, François.......	1	8	36–55
Cavilier, J., f.m.c.......	1	6	36–55	Datty, Anne..........	2	8	36–55
Packet, J. B., f.m.c.....	11	21	55–100	Coutan, Rosette........	6	15	24–36
				Barthelemi, François....	1	9	36–55
LAFAYETTE				Barthelemi, Paul........	4	12	36–55
Mathew, Joseph........	2	3	36–55	POINT COUPEE			
Darby, Celestin.........	2	10	24–36	Marimat, Madame......	7	8	36–55
				Delhonde, Sophie......	38	48	36–55
NATCHITOCHES				Destrehaus fils, Honori..	10	11	10–24
Btaue, John Bt........	1	3	10–24	Decuire, Lefroix........	59	71	24–36
Cloutier, Augustin......	1	8	36–55	Pauche, V.............	1	7	24–36
Rachal, Pier............	4	11	36–55	Bonfois, Charles........	1	6	24–36
Balthasar, Louis........	2	4	10–24	Curiel, Joseph..........	40	44	36–55
Rachal, John Bt........	6	17	36–55	Decuire, Antoine........	70	76	36–55
Birt, Asaac............	5	11	10–24	Decond, Sostin.........	10	14	24–36
Dueprie, Phillip........	2	5	24–36	Pawk, Jasin...........	3	4	36–55
Metgier, Naciest........	1	6	24–36	Decond, Noré..........	1	5	55–100
Free, Batteart..........	1	3	55–100	Severin, Leandre........	60	68	36–55
Meytoier, John Bt. Dom.	3	12	24–36	Escoe, Lewis...........	1	4	36–55
Meytoier, Domnick.....	25	38	55–100	Perrau, Henriette.......	1	3	55–100
Meytoier, Joseph.......	13	21	36–55	Albert, Sallie..........	1	3	36–55
Meytoier, Fils (?), Fran-				Duperon, Victor........	10	26	55–100
cies................	2	6	10–24	De Crosier, Augustin....	1	2	36–55
Meytoier, Francies, Sr...	5	9	36–55	Key, Lucindy..........	1	4	24–36
Meytoier Augustin, John							
Bt...............	13	23	24–36	ST. BERNARD			
Meytoier, Louis........	54	66	55–100	Louis.................	6	7	36–55
Meytoier, Augustin.....	54	60	55–100				
Meytoier, Ogest (?).....	13	19	24–36	ST. CHARLES			
Meytoier, Susan........	20	21	55–100	Fatil, Baptist..........	3	5	36–55
Meytoier, Agsile.......	3	8	24–36	Sabatier, Severs........	1	7	36–55
Meytoier, Pier, Junior...	8	16	55–100	Augustin, Eloise........	8	15	36–55
Meytoier, Pier, Sr.......	2	5	10–24	D'Arensbourg, Gilbert...	1	7	24–36
Lariece, Manieuel.......	4	11	24–36	Honoré, Gabriel........	3	10	24–36
Larcos, Margriet.......	4	9	55–100	Richoux, Joseph........	2	9	36–55
Larvean, Joseph........	1	5	10–24	Oldélaide..............	1	5	55–100
Monett, Louis..........	1	5	10–24	Molière................	10	14	36–55
Rock, Saraham.........	12	21	24–36	ST. JOHN BAPTISTE			
Samper (?), Jerom......	3	9	36–55	Villeré, Ve· E., Negse· Lib.	3	17	55–100
Dupas, Ameal..........	3	8	24–36	Rillieux, Ve· Fai· (?).....	49	62	55–100
Cottonmie, Atonine.....	3	7	36–55	Deslondes, Victoire......	52	77	36–55
Corner, Florentine......	16	24	24–36	Ferrand, C., & St· St· Dus-			
Lamote, Louis..........	4	12	55–100	nan.................	38	49	36–55
Cemore, Charles........	8	15	36–55	Isidor, Auge...........	1	15	36–55
Grasp, Elijah...........	3	13	24–36	ST. LANDRY			
Trichel, Joseph L........	1	6	24–36	Frilat, Louis...........	5	11	36–55
Trichel, Joeann.........	2	5	36–55	Bernard, Victoire.......	1	5	24–36
Rochet, Suset..........	6	14	55–100				

LOUISIANA—Continued

Name	Slaves	Total	Age	Name	Slaves	Total	Age
Opelousas				ST. MARTIN			
Baldwin, Manon........	1	3	36–55	*St. Martinsville*			
Lange, Leonora.........	2	7	36–55	Fontenette, Eloise.......	3	10	24–36
Peignier, Françoise......	1	3	55–100	Delahoupage, Isador....	3	7	55–100
				Lenormand, Martin.....	44	54	55–100
Belleview				Chalinette (Osene)......	1	9	55–100
Malveau, Laurent.......	18	26	55–100	Lavillebeune, Charles....	1	14	55–100
Malveau, Baptiste......	4	13	36–55	Grevernberg, Celestin ...	2	9	55–100
				Vils, Philip.............	6	14	24–36
Plaquemine Brulé				Fontenette, Lénon......	4	15	36–55
Donatto, Martin........	75	87	55–100	Lenormand, Ursin.......	13	19	36–55
Boulard, Jambe.........	3	6	24–36	Lenormand. Char^{te}.....	14	19	55–100
				Champagne, F.........	1	7	24–36
Grand Prairie				Lenormand, Norbert....	18	20	36–55
Fontinot, Louis A. B.....	4	5	36–55				
George, Baptiste........	4	10	24–36	ST. MARY			
				Pinta, Casemir.........	2	10	24–36
Prairie Maumont				Frillot, Aimé...........	3	13	24–36
Fontinot, Augustin B....	7	14	55–100	Boutté, Philipeau.......	10	15	55–100
Simon, Veuve Louis.....	8	10	36–55	Verdin, Leon...........	4	15	24–36
				Verdin, Romain........	8	24	36–55
Bayou Mallet				Charlete, B^{te}., Do.......	2	5	36–55
Simeon, François........	2	7	24–36	Olivier, Magdelaine.....	1	11	55–100
				Olivier, Adelaide........	4	9	36–55
Coteau of Church Prairie							
Lamelle, François.......	7	21	36–55	ST. TAMMANY			
Bolan, Veuve George....	6	7	36–55	Brasier, Maxilion........	1	4	36–55
Paillitte, Antoine.......	8	16	55–100	Brockston, Phillip.......	1	4	36–55
Villier, Marie...........	1	3	55–100	Popelous, Cassimer.....	1	8	36–55
Thiery, Louis, père......	3	5	24–36	Baham, Voltaire........	1	3	24–36
				Baham, Pierre..........	1	5	24–36
Quelquesui				Baham, Seymore........	2	4	10–24
Johnson, John..........	4	8	24–36	Maxon, Roselle........	7	11	55–100
Ashworth, Jesse.........	1	11	36–55	Raby, Antoine..........	1	3	36–55
Carrillo, Joseph........	1	9	55–100	Baham, Mary Ann......	6	15	36–55
Bayou Mallet				TERRE BONNE			
Guillory, Jean B........	18	32	55–100	Billeaux, Etienne.......	5	10	36–55
Donat, Auguste.........	4	6	24–36				
Simeon, George.........	1	10	36–55	WASHITA (OUACHITA)			
Charlow, Jacques.......	5	8	55–100	Watts, Joseph..........	8	21	36–55
				Jerod, Francis..........	33	42	24–36
Bayou Teche				WEST BATON ROUGE			
Osanne, Valarien........	27	38	36–55	Alsire, Helene..........	3	8	36–55
Lesassier, Jean..........	19	27	36–55	Detreant, Mrs. Honoré..	2	4	36–55
Balqué, Joseph, père....	18	21	36–55	Demonel, Terance......	6	15	100–
Balqué, Joseph, fils......	1	8	24–36	Hubaut, Charles........	1	3	36–55
Muillion, Jean B........	52	57	55–100	Bienville, Julien........	6	14	24–36
Lamelle, Narcisse.......	8	13	10–24	Recard, Saint Luke.....	16	21	55–100
Lamelle, Marie Jeanne..	8	11	55–100	Recard, Widow Mary ...	11	19	10–24
Gallo, Jean.............	12	16	24–36	Rapelier, James.........	9	18	36–55
Lafleur, Baptiste........	3	6	55–100	Hubaut, Leopold.... ..	1	3	36–55
Valliere, Louis..........	4	11	24–36	Honoré Fils............	30	38	36–55
Papillion, Alexander.....	1	7	24–36	Polen Verret...........	69	74	36–55
Cofine, Felicite.........	3	5	55–100				
Bass, James............	5	10	10–24	PARISH OF ST. JAMES			
Sweat, Guilbert.........	4	5	55–100	—ACADIA			
Fontineau, Juinerice B...	4	6	24–36	Nemorin Rhodanez......	3	6	24–36

LOUISIANA—*Continued*

Name	Slaves	Total	Age	Name	Slaves	Total	Age
NEW ORLEANS CITY				Canuel, Julien	1	5	55–100
Inhabitants included be-				Rochon, Rosette	2	7	55–100
tween Rampart Street, the				Brulée, Similien	5	10	55–100
new burying ground and							
the Basin				*Between Esplanade St. &*			
Labretonnière, M. L.	3	8	36–55	*Canal Marigny*			
				Populus Doroté	1	4	24–36
Between the Basin and				Françoise, Maria	1	10	55–100
Bayou Road				Fondale	1	6	36–55
Braquemart, Victoire....	1	9	36–55	Beauguis, F^cis.	3	11	36–55
Dupré, Celeste	3	6	36–55	Fanchon, F^cise·	1	5	36–55
Ramos, Philippe	2	6	24–36	Jeune, Raimond Gaillard	1	3	55–100
Rost, Edouard	1	5	24–36	Duval, Annette	1	6	36–55
Roy, Usanie	1	3	36–55	Marquet, Lewis	1	4	24–36
Porté, F^cis.	1	8	36–55	Beauvais, Marie	1	4	24–36
Forneret, Joseph	3	8	36–55	Villard, Marie Louisa....	1	6	36–55
Coursel, Martil	2	4	24–36	Dupart, Clerck	7	12	24–36
Gallo, Widow Noel	1	3	36–55	Moreau, Manuel	3	10	24–36
Caulbet, Widow	1	5	55–100	Borré, Madeleine	6	8	55–100
Montrose, N^as·	4	17	55–100	Jounin, Cadet	1	3	24–36
				Gallo, Lewis	2	7	55–100
Between Bayou Rd. and				Coquillot, Noël	1	3	36–55
the Lake				Flecheu, Hennry	1	4	24–36
Obry, Marguerite	3	9	55–100	Jourdan, W^dow· Celestin	1	7	36–55
				Fouchet, Odele	2	7	55–100
Between Bayou Road &				Parilliat, Margueritte....	4	8	36–55
l'Amour St.				Burel, Achille	1	6	36–55
Hazur, Prosper	3	11	36–55	Taguin, Harnot	3	4	55–100
Dauphin, W^dow·	9	15	36–55	Plaissy, A.	5	12	24–36
Lavaux, Jarde	3	6	36–55	Lajoncière, Celestine....	1	6	24–36
Cheval, Paul	3	7	55–100	Félicié, John Peter	1	6	24–36
Renald, Aug^te·	4	10	24–36	Perrillioto, Joseph	4	5	55–100
Rebauld	3	5	24–36	Francis	1	3	24–36
Rilieux, Elizié	2	7	24–36	Guenon, Hursin	2	9	36–55
Duverlet, F^cis.	2	9	24–36	Macartis, Sophie	4	6	36–55
Metsinger, Benedique ...	1	5	36–55	Thérèse	2	3	36–55
Dolliole, Joseph	5	7	36–55	St. Amant, Eloise	2	6	24–36
Azur, Marcelite	4	8	24–36	Etienne, Louisa	4	10	55–100
Magnac, Charles	1	7	55–100	Mariux	1	9	36–55
Hurtin, Felicianna	1	3	10–24	Popotte	3	7	36–55
Chapdu, Caroline	2	6	24–36	Dautelonne, M. C.	8	14	36–55
Duval, Salinette	1	8	36–55	Mercier, Seraphine	2	9	36–55
Enard, Simeon	1	5	24–36	Justine	4	11	55–100
Juliette	2	9	10–24	Lambert, Richard	1	6	24–36
Decoudwux, Chares.	2	7	55–100				
Lavarie, Joseph, Son....	2	11	10–24	*Between Canal Marigny*			
Bordier, Petronie	3	7	55–100	*& Monderville St.*			
Pernet, Madelaine	2	5	36–55	Simon, Constance	3	5	55–100
Obry, Zelia	1	7	24–36	Deberque, Constantin ...	1	8	24–36
Bellouard, John	3	6	24–36				
Lajoie, Julien	1	9	55–100	*Monderville St. & Fau-*			
Madelaine	2	4	55–100	*bourg Donois*			
Constance	2	9	55–100	Benjamen, Anthony	2	8	36–55
L'amour St. between				Joseph, Bazile	1	3	36–55
Esplanade St. & the Canal				Maria	3	5	36–55
Marigny							
Azur, Isidor	1	10	36–55				

LOUISIANA—*Continued*

Name	Slaves	Total	Age	Name	Slaves	Total	Age
Monderville St.				Smith, Hellen..........	1	3	24–36
Fbg. Marigny &				Montgomery, Charles ...	2	4	55–100
Fbg. Donois				Clement, Richard.......	1	3	36–55
Aubertine.............	2	6	24–36	Moore, William.........	6	12	55–100
Zamor, Madeleine......	2	7	55–100	Gravier, Joseph.........	1	3	36–55
Fouché, Nelson........	3	8	24–36	Bonseigneur, Arsene.....	1	12	10–24
Salbrier, Patry........	1	8	24–36	Villemont, Josephine....	1	4	55–100
Laurent, W^dow.......	2	4	36–55	Bonseigneur, Nerestan...	1	7	24–36
Casimir, W^dow.......	1	3	36–55	Key, Richard..........	1	2	24–36
Petitgeot, F^cis.........	2	5	36–55	Moise, Justine..........	6	8	36–55
Lachaise, Catherine.....	2	9	36–55	Francis, George.........	1	3	24–36
Doublet, Maurice......	1	4	10–24	Cazot, Jean............	4	7	36–55
Lacroix...............	2	4	24–36	Pierre, Elisa...........	2	4	24–36
Compigny, J. L........	1	6	55–100	Claire, Marie..........	1	2	55–100
Blouin, Augustin.......	4	13	36–55	Sepine, F.............	2	8	36–55
Denaux, Anne..........	3	12	36–55	Nicholas, Jenny........	1	2	36–55
				Jolibois, Genevieve......	3	4	36–55
Upper Suburbs of New				Mathieu, Valmont......	1	5	24–36
Orleans				Boyer, Lucy............	4	8	36–55
Josspot, J. S...........	1	2	24–36	Desvignes, Hellen.......	1	4	24–36
Diggs, James..........	2	4	10–24	Patty.................	6	8	36–55
Smith, Peggy..........	4	6	36–55	Dupas, Mary..........	1	3	36–55
Herman...............	2	4	36–55	Teta, Louis...........	5	7	36–55
Kelan, Phillip.........	3	4	36–55	Jenkins, Edward........	3	9	55–100
Samba, Marie-louise.....	4	10	55–100	Hilaire, Rosine.........	3	4	36–55
Carlon, Etienne........	1	5	24–36	Hardy, Jaques..........	6	8	36–55
Chalambert, M^rie· J^ne· ..	1	6	55–100	Robert, Louverain......	2	10	36–55
Beaulieu, Guilbert......	1	9	24–36	Lacöesse, Pierre........	1	5	24–36
Hartfield, J^h...........	1	8	24–36	Reymond, Pierre.......	1	5	24–36
Sirnmons, Sophia.......	1	3	10–24	Garcia, Pierre.........	2	10	36–55
Guyonesse, Baptiste.....	4	10	36–55	Lawrence, Francis......	1	7	36–55
White, Charlotte.......	2	6	55–100	Botts, Cupids.........	3	5	36–55
Smith, Henry..........	2	6	36–55	Escaut, Antoine........	1	8	36–55
Elley, John...........	2	4	24–36	Brown................	2	5	36–55
Baden, Rémond........	6	8	24–36	Smith, Becky..........	1	2	24–36
Garaut, Rose..........	2	16	100–	Degruys, François......	1	2	24–36
Smith, Thomas........	3	6	55–100	Thomas, Flora.........	1	3	36–55
Francis, John..........	2	3	55–100	Hashpy, Nelson........	1	2	36–55
Edward, Stephen.......	1	2	10–24	Bresky, Jacob..........	2	5	24–36
Smith, Diana..........	3	9	55–100	Duval, Gaston.........	1	8	24–36
Jonau, Antoine........	8	14	24–36	Monnery, Mrs. A.......	1	14	24–36
Dunn, James..........	2	5	36–55	Barnabé, J^n· B^te·......	3	5	36–55
Vembles, Jacob........	1	9	36–55	Divivier, Louise........	17	18	55–100
Bouté, François P......	1	4	24–36	Manuishon, Jacob.....	5	10	36–55
Elliot, Maria..........	2	3	10–24	Dupuis, Mrs...........	4	7	36–55
Dauphin, Pelagie......	3	11	36–55	Béguin, Agathe........	2	4	36–55
Johnson, Anna.........	2	5	36–55	Tinsley, Nancy........	7	11	24–36
Henriette.............	3	4	36–55	Augustin, Aimee.......	2	5	24–36
Antoine, Baptiste......	1	6	24–36	Asquier, J^n· Louis......	3	10	55–100
Isidor, Telside.........	1	2	24–36	Escaut, Louison........	4	14	55–100
Woods, George........	1	4	36–55	Casson, Pulchérie.......	2	7	36–55
Johnson, William P.....	1	3	24–36	Gaudin, Pelagie........	1	3	55–100
Grammont, Jean.......	1	3	24–36	St. Amant, Louis	1	9	24–36
Boutimé, François.....	2	8	24–36	Gougis, Leda..........	2	7	24–36
Keating, Ann B........	1	3	10–24	Cabaret, Marguerite.....	2	4	24–36
Filié, Pierre...........	1	7	36–55	Craig, James..........	1	4	36–55
Champio, Victoire.....	2	13	55–100	Hamelin, Julien.........	1	10	36–55

LOUISIANA—*Continued*

Name	Slaves	Total	Age	Name	Slaves	Total	Age
Upper Suburbs of New				Calvin, Pierre	1	9	100–
Orleans—Cont.				S^t· Toëguo (?), Polenar..	4	9	55–100
Laurent, Pierre	3	8	36–55	Chadirac, Miss Fany....	2	8	36–55
Porée, Charles, Sen	2	11	55–100	Priet, Henriette	3	14	36–55
Formorette, Pierre	1	5	24–36	Valentin, Fran^s·	1	6	36–55
Dauphin, Catische	5	12	36–55	Girardeau, Bruno	1	5	24–36
Baque, Zelmire	2	5	36–55	Pelerin, Modeste	6	14	36–55
Grandmaison, Sanite....	13	16	55–100	Borry, Ursin	1	10	36–55
Lioteau, Pierre	2	4	36–55	Perrauta, Savinien	4	8	36–55
Mallet, Augustin	1	6	55–100	Lathrope, Eulalie	6	14	36–55
Deale, Marie Thereze....	3	10	36–55	Faury, Miss Antoinette..	4	10	36–55
Miniche, Orphise	1	3	10–24	Populus, Ant.	7	11	36–55
Borée, Paul	4	9	55–100	Marias, P^rre· Ch^s·	1	8	36–55
Macarty, Jason	4	8	55–100	Lebouh, Marie Victoire..	5	8	36–55
Descuirs, Françoise	2	6	36–55	Garridel, Miss Fanny....	3	6	24–36
Flemming, Jean	2	5	24–36	Lambert (?), Jean	3	9	24–36
Dimba (?), Phillips	4	7	36–55	Gencau, Rosette	4	6	55–100
Savoie, Françoise	2	12	55–100	St. Ourse, Oursine	3	9	36–55
Sterling, Rose	1	4	24–36	Dalby, Celeste	2	10	36–55
Fortier, Etienne	4	12	36–55	Angnant, Louise S^t·	1	4	36–55
Fleuriau, Mannette	2	5	55–100	Birot, Piron	1	12	36–55
Doriaucourt, Marianne..	1	2	55–100	Bourdilles, Ursule	3	7	36–55
Bacchus, Eulalie	2	14	55–100	Cheval, Leandre	1	8	36–55
Percy, Héloise	5	11	55–100	Mortimer, Pepite	1	6	55–100
Apollon, Jaques	1	2	36–55	Borrys, L. A.	4	14	36–55
Fabre, Françoise	5	8	36–55	Brion, A.	5	15	36–55
Frère, Rosette	4	13	36–55	Savary, M.	2	13	36–55
Pierce, George	5	6	36–55	Besson, A.	1	9	24–36
Manice, Blaise	1	8	36–55	Bizotte, F^se·	1	6	24–36
Nourice, Marie	1	3	36–55	Anoreaux (?), S^te·	1	8	55–100
Lewis, Charlotte, Miss...	1	3	36–55	Roviaux, Judique	4	13	24–36
S^t· Amand, Mme· Hen-				Hardouin, Eugenie	4	13	36–55
riette	1	2	10–24	Laroche, Victoire	1	8	36–55
Azur, Philip	3	4	55–100	Davier, Carmelite	6	14	55–100
Dasincourt, Maurice....	1	10	36–55	Navard, Modeste	4	10	36–55
Lafitte, Guillaume	1	5	24–36	Purdom, Narcisse	3	12	36–55
Bumchartrean, Melle·H^tte·	2	10	36–55	Duforge, Cantrelle	11	18	55–100
Alexandre, Cata	1	4	24–36	Murat, Gaston	7	18	55–100
Ross, Edouard	1	3	36–55	Derbanne, Alcide	3	11	36–55
Victor, Joseph S^t·	2	3	36–55	Silva, François	1	7	36–55
Cavillier, Miss Catherine.	5	9	36–55	Bonseigneur, J. B.	1	7	24–36
Arnaud, Leandre	1	4	36–55	Pinta, Danatien	1	9	24–36
Bozan, Miss Annette....	1	6	55–100	Gabriel, Sanon	4	11	36–55
Raby, Rodolph	4	5	36–55	Maurivez, D.	4	12	36–55
Dubranel (Charles)	2	8	36–55	Danache, Ch^s·	5	15	55–100
Jolly, Urbain	1	6	36–55	Rachal, Lucien	5	14	36–55
Campanel, B.	3	8	36–55	Auvergne, Philip	5	14	36–55
Legardeur, Charlot	1	10	55–100	Neuville, Ant.	2	7	24–36
McCarty, Cécée	32	38	24–36	Vivier, Ch^s·	4	15	55–100
Borel, Miss Melanie	4	8	36–55	Hopkins, Cicilia	2	6	24–36
Chan, Adolphe	2	5	10–24	Macarty, Brigite	3	5	24–36
Lavinsandier, Charlotte .	5	11	36–55	Macoste, Widow Desire..	6	17	24–36
Mondelly, Sanon	3	5	36–55	Christophe, Firmin	1	7	24–36
Andre, Mortimer	1	6	36–55	Pierron, Zelime	1	7	24–36
ArtheBuys, Gustave.	1	5	55–100	Cavanard, Lolote	4	7	55–100
Guiramond, Barite	1	8	36–55	Perdron, Eloise	3	9	24–36
Mandeville, Judique	1	13	36–55	Ambroises, T. B.	2	8	24–36

LOUISIANA—*Continued*

Name	Slaves	Total	Age	Name	Slaves	Total	Age
Upper Suburbs of New Orleans—Cont.				Dubruny, Edouard......	1	6	24–36
				Plantevigne, V.........	7	15	100–
Ferron, Modeste........	2	9	36–55	Macarty, H.............	6	8	24–36
Pavis, André...........	7	17	55–100	Guiramand, R..........	3	7	36–55
Toutant, Amelie........	1	6	55–100	Seressole, Lˢ·..........	3	12	36–55
Lafoste, Eglé...........	2	5	24–36	Arnaud, Mimie.........	3	10	36–55
Barbet, Celeste........	3	7	36–55	Berrard, N. B..........	3	6	10–24
Rochiblane, Rochebrune.	7	10	36–55	Sennette, A...........	1	8	36–55
Angelique, Widow......	4	7	36–55	Duhart, Ant..........	3	6	36–55
Gourge, Poupone.......	4	9	55–100	Joublotte, Sanite.......	3	13	36–55
Prauvert, Cephise......	7	11	10–24	Laroche, Josephine.....	1	6	24–36
Barbe, M...............	2	6	24–36	Garriques, Louise.......	2	14	100–
Vermillon (?), Eulalie....	2	10	55–100	Maurice, Jeannette.....	1	5	24–36
Canfran, Misse........	10	17	36–55	Anodin, M. B..........	2	6	36–55
Dalez, Estelle..........	1	5	36–55	Joseph, Marie.........	2	10	36–55
Benite, Michel..........	3	12	36–55	Volunt, Mimite........	10	21	55–100
Lefebre, Eugenie........	9	16	36–55	Gayard, Poupone.......	1	8	36–55
Donaut, Henri..........	6	9	36–55	Gerard, Rosalie........	1	8	36–55
Votaire, Maurice.......	2	13	36–55	Bertholl, Eugenie.......	3	9	24–36
Levasseur, Mirabin.....	4	10	36–55	Arnaud, Gertrude.......	5	7	55–100
Feron, Marie Dastuge...	1	12	55–100	Thomas, Widow R.....	5	11	36–55
Liautaud, Elize........	4	14	36–55	Cordeviolle, Ignace.....	2	7	36–55
Claiborne, Augustin....	1	9	24–36	Lusignan, Valsin........	7	18	36–55
Baulos, Hortaire.......	4	11	55–100	Zenon, Lˢ· A............	2	5	24–36
Montelle, Mimie.......	2	6	36–55	Clair, Margᵗᵉ· Sᵗ·.....	3	17	55–100
Ganucheau, Annette.....	2	13	55–100	Mammes, Helene.......	1	7	100–
Laborde, Joseph........	2	10	36–55	Cezain, Tymothée.......	1	12	55–100
Dafauchard, Louis.....	1	8	55–100	Frumence, F............	2	9	36–55
Ursin, Magnola.........	2	9	24–36	Clement, Cécille........	3	11	55–100
Legardeur, Adrien......	3	12	55–100	Sosthene, F............	1	2	36–55
Lerond, Henriette.......	7	16	55–100	Josse, Adelaide........	7	17	55–100
Honoré, Elizabeth......	1	8	55–100	Dorothe, Agathe........	1	8	36–55
Casabon, Widow........	3	10	36–55	Sévérin, Apauline......	2	11	55–100
Garcin, Iris............	4	11	55–100	Zacharie, Euphrasie.....	3	11	55–100
Roche, Athalie.........	1	6	24–36	Prudent, Zenon.......	5	9	24–36
Salcas, Fillette..........	2	6	36–55	Athanase (Desiree)......	11	21	55–100
Maurin, Cécé...........	5	9	36–55	Pascal, Isidore..........	1	4	24–36
Cornelius, Amelie......	3	9	36–55	Urbain, Jeanne.........	9	20	55–100
Charbonnet, Celeste.....	3	11	55–100	Hildevert, Philip.......	1	4	24–36
Caillavette, Aristide.....	4	14	36–55	Maximin, Germain......	4	10	55–100
Legardeur, Arthur......	1	7	55–100	Nérée, Petronille.......	2	5	36–55
Lemoine, Bauvais.......	5	21	36–55	Silvere, Gervais........	2	9	36–55
Torame, Charles.......	5	13	55–100	Isidore, Prosper........	9	16	55–100
Magloire, Donatien.....	2	7	55–100	Bajolaire, R. E.........	8	19	55–100
Mathurin, Auguste......	4	17	55–100	Perdreaux, Clovis.......	1	6	36–55
Sidney, Louis...........	1	12	55–100	Fernand, Gérard........	1	9	24–36
Anathol, Cyprien.......	2	11	36–55	Raymond, Adolphe.....	4	10	24–36
Morrison, Chaˢ·........	2	14	55–100	Brodequin, Marie.......	6	15	55–100
Pontier, Francˢ·........	9	19	55–100	Dorfeuelle, Maria.......	2	6	55–100
Dunand, Chˢ·..........	4	14	55–100	Schmidt, J. R..........	2	9	24–36
Perdreau, Maurice......	4	15	55–100	Le Chaste, Aristide.....	1	5	24–36
Jouacinthe, Ralph......	3	12	36–55	Joviolle, Henriette......	5	15	36–55
Candide, Théo..........	1	10	24–36	Duperrier, Daniel.......	10	21	36–55
Pargon, Barth..........	4	13	55–100	Vassant, Celestin.......	3	15	55–100
Ponponneau, Clara......	5	17	36–55	Pavien, Louis..........	1	10	36–55
Leclair, Jos.............	2	7	36–55	Tallarey, Eugenie.......	5	12	24–36
Gueringer, Ant.........	5	16	55–100	Sᵗ· Amand, M. J........	5	10	24–36

LOUISIANA--*Continued*

Name	Slaves	Total	Age	Name	Slaves	Total	Age
Upper Suburbs of New Orleans—Cont.				Lapitto, Marie Rose.....	4	10	36–55
				Villard, Catiche.........	5	12	36–55
André, Magdelaine......	1	6	36–55	Durand, Pierre.........	6	13	36–55
Tervallon, F...........	2	5	24–36	Toussine, Marie........	5	14	36–55
Rousseau, Widow P.....	1	5	36–55	Dufrene, Jean Lˢ.......	5	9	24–36
Dupré, Eulalie..........	2	5	36–55	Mirbel, Neuris..........	6	17	55–100
Baudin, Génevieve.....	2	9	55–100	Merieux, Agathe........	3	11	24–36
Dupiton, Widow........	3	10	55–100	Mangonna, Virginie.....	10	20	36–55
Lamotte, Wid...........	2	6	36–55	Fournier, Camille.......	5	13	36–55
Duharlet, Rose.........	4	12	36–55	Roques, Derchal........	11	23	55–100
Guirot, Claudine........	5	13	36–55	Wilfride, Caliste........	4	14	24–36
Fusillier, F.............	1	4	55–100	Gayac, Anathole........	2	9	55–100
Trevigne, Garçon.......	1	7	10–24	Raphael, Hyacinthe.....	8	10	24–36
Rouppon, Pierre........	13	19	24–36	Maurille, Euphemie.....	1	4	24–36
Lataure, Severin........	6	13	24–36	Rigobert, Geneviève.....	16	23	36–55
Gabrielle, Chˢ..........	2	10	55–100	Gordien, Desire.........	3	15	55–100
Laire, M. Annette.......	4	11	55–100	Sabas, Olympe.........	1	7	24–36
Montreuille, Félicitié....	1	3	55–100	Delphin, Ives...........	5	15	36–55
Roubioux, Rosette......	3	15	55–100	Péprin, Aglae..........	4	12	55–100
Colvis, F..............	1	4	36–55	Urbain, Jeanne.........	1	4	36–55
Maurin, Bellone........	4	7	55–100	Leufroy, John..........	6	14	36–55
Tessier, Sanite.........	8	14	55–100	Paulin, Alexis..........	1	6	24–36
Dauphin, Marie........	7	14	55–100	Aplanas, Meonide.......	2	7	10–24
Andry, Seraphine.......	8	15	55–100	Lanoix, Rose...........	13	23	36–55
Lacroix, Pierre..........	2	15	55–100	Savary, Emile..........	8	16	55–100
Alexis, Eglée..........	1	9	55–100	Dersac, Ignace.........	4	14	55–100
St. Amand, Sophie......	5	13	36–55	Bourgoin, Pierre........	2	7	36–55
Dizt, Gustave..........	2	11	24–36	Lacoste, Pedronille......	4	12	24–36
Lancellay, Jerome.......	1	2	36–55	Macédone, Thérèse.....	4	12	36–55
Imbert, Eleanore........	1	5	36–55	Sévérin, Agathe........	1	7	24–36
Dugunge, Amelie.......	3	10	55–100	Gaudry, Estelle.........	4	13	55–100
Lafferiere, B............	2	9	36–55	Dudley, Alphonse.......	2	4	36–55
Lahoussey, Simon.......	3	11	24–36	Mothélose, Gabriel.....	11	25	55–100
Laborde, Uranie........	1	7	36–55	Régio, Antoinette.......	2	6	24–36
Daw, Camille..........	1	7	55–100	Pargroux, Zénon........	1	9	55–100
Borel, Chˢ· Lˢ·..........	2	15	36–55	Raquet, Antoinette......	8	18	55–100
Janvier, Ursin..........	1	6	24–36	Crosait, Lisida..........	2	4	24–36
Vivant, Louison........	10	23	55–100	Hospineta, Julie........	5	10	24–36
White, Palmin..........	1	4	36–55	Franck, Adelaide........	1	2	24–36
Bourjon, André.........	3	16	55–100	Bronze, Judique........	3	9	24–36
Chatelain, Carlos.......	4	15	36–55	Bajoliere, Edouard.....	7	14	36–55
Latapie, Poupone.......	2	10	55–100	Bruno, Edme...........	1	8	55–100
Magloire, Juliens.......	2	5	36–55	Roupelin, Osmin........	2	7	36–55
Burthe, Benjamin.......	9	22	55–100	Cabaret, Joseph........	9	12	55–100
Casbin, Pierre..........	3	8	24–36	Parvis, Cécille..........	7	10	24–36
Latiolet, Magdelaine....	4	11	55–100	Lesenne, Adeline........	1	3	24–36
Teyoval, Judique.......	5	9	36–55	Deléandre, Géneviève ...	3	11	55–100
Montarler, Désirée......	9	20	55–100	Foureade, M............	1	5	36–55
Blinval, Adolphe........	3	6	36–55	Auguste Jé, François....	6	12	36–55
Laborde, Eulalie........	8	17	55–100	Wiltz, Victoire..........	1	5	36–55
Purdon, Avelina........	1	4	24–36	Bullie, Widow C........	3	13	36–55
Rahton (?), Marguerite..	1	8	24–36	Ducraix, Marianne......	1	5	36–55
Gofte, Adolphe.........	3	15	55–100	Amoth., Widow.........	2	6	100–
Espagnette, Marie Charlotte...............	3	10	36–55	Fromentin, Françoise....	1	8	55–100
Saulet, Felicite.........	1	8	36–55	Bierra, Rose...........	5	12	36–55
Mandeville, Eulalie.....	13	17	36–55	Guillaume, Toussaint....	8	13	24–36
				Lonny, Luce...........	2	11	24–36

LOUISIANA—Continued

Name	Slaves	Total	Age	Name	Slaves	Total	Age
Upper Suburbs of New Orleans—Cont.				Delille, Felix	2	5	24–36
				Séjour, Louis	3	10	36–55
Corbet, Julien	1	6	36–55	Bordeaux, Jeanne	2	8	36–55
Timpêgue, Louis A.	2	9	24–36	Renald, Mimie	1	7	55–100
Castillon, Victor	9	19	55–100	Dubreiulle (?), Marie	1	2	24–36
Sully (?), C	4	13	36–55	Castanette, Suzette	1	5	24–36
Lacoste, Constance	3	12	36–55	Baptiste, Alexandrine	1	5	55–100
Maurin, Poupone	3	11	24–36	Perodin, Wid.	1	2	36–55
Seradin, Antoinette	4	10	24–36	Celestin, Widow	4	13	55–100
Menas, Stephanie	1	2	10–24	Lefevre, Jacques	3	5	55–100
Etienne, Widow	4	15	55–100	Miller, Caroline	13	14	24–36
Fortuné, Bonnie	3	10	36–55	Larday, Fanchette	5	15	55–100
Dupuy, Mgne.	11	15	24–36	Legon, Ariste	4	9	24–36
Legian, Fs	1	3	24–36	Noël, Marie	6	18	55–100
Gouengo, Irene	2	4	24–36	Armand, Modeste	1	4	24–36
Barbe, Miss	3	4	10–24	Lagrange, Depit	2	7	36–55
Rivert, Constce.	17	20	55–100	Duperain, M.	6	15	36–55
D'Emart, Me.	2	8	36–55	Ménadier, Rose	6	9	24–36
Gayard, Sr., Rd.	6	10	55–100	Gronge, Savarie	4	14	36–55
DuBois, Eulalie	4	10	10–24	Blois, Edmond	2	8	24–36
Legoesler, Erasme	4	9	36–55	Mercier, Felix	2	9	36–55
Bluzeau, Pierre	1	5	36–55	Arsene, Désirée	1	9	36–55
Maurin, Merandine	3	4	24–36	Evrard, Omer	4	9	36–55
Rosine, M.	1	10	55–100	Flavien, Noël	1	4	24–36
Marcus, Eloise	2	12	55–100	Benoist, Ursin	4	10	36–55
Reytre, Jeannette	1	2	24–36	Bénétaud, Estelle	4	11	36–55
Barbet, Cloë	2	3	10–24	Landrin, Mathieu	6	20	55–100
Barbet, Delphine	1	2	10–24	Néréaud, Benjamin	2	10	36–55
Borosée, Fred	2	4	55–100	Lueguarde, Bazile	1	7	55–100
Cabaret, Lise	2	13	36–55	Martial, A.	1	4	24–36
Valentin, François	4	15	24–36	Castiaux, Bern. (?)	3	10	36–55
Lanna, Désire	1	4	24–36	Daquin, Silvain	5	10	36–55
Deribon, Widow	1	6	36–55	Dalché, Louise	1	3	24–36
Tounence, Zizite	4	6	24–36	Chery, Chistée	1	4	36–55
Boutin, Victorine	3	10	24–36	Linguo, Alexandrine	1	12	36–55
Guilbaut, Josephine	1	6	55–100	Camisac, Résinette	1	5	24–36
Maurin, Charlotte	6	18	36–55	Laurent, Wid. St.	3	6	55–100
Montford, Heliopolis	4	18	36–55	Lange, Florisse	2	10	36–55
Hilaire, N. A.	7	15	36–55	Vilmo, Wid. Celeste	2	4	36–55
Bougère, Rosette	2	11	36–55	Gautreau, B.	2	9	55–100
Nicholas, Popote	1	3	10–24	Caiblet, Ben	4	13	55–100
Borbeau, Noel	1	5	55–100	Ferraud, Celestin	2	5	24–36
Forestal, Pauline	2	6	24–36	Coussin, Marie	2	8	36–55
Lagrange, Adelle	3	7	55–100	Cheridan, Emiliana	3	7	55–100
Foucher, Modeste	1	12	36–55	Jerreau, Thêodule	6	14	36–55
Pradex, Rosiette	2	9	36–55	Daboval, Jules	1	5	36–55
Duehemin, Aimée	2	4	36–55	Bernard, Guillme.	5	6	36–55
Cambre, Thérèse	1	3	36–55	Saramon, Henriette	1	7	100–
Montreuille, Monon	3	7	36–55	Labruyère, Désirée	1	13	55–100
Leon, Thos.	2	7	24–36	André, Judice	2	5	36–55
Mayero, Toussine	2	5	36–55	Poinset, Thémire	5	13	36–55
Bertheno, Laïsse	2	8	24–36	Duchesne, Ferd.	1	3	24–36
D'Arneville, Pelagie	4	16	100–	Montamar, V. A.	1	5	55–100
Talhand, Pierre	2	10	24–36	Piron, Emélie	2	8	36–55
Aubert, Elizabeth	3	10	55–100	Cobet, Caliste	1	8	24–36
Gentilles, Lse.	1	4	24–36	Bienaimee, B.	1	7	36–55
Durel, Justine	1	6	36–55	Duraine, Jean	5	16	55–100

LOUISIANA—*Continued*

Name	Slaves	Total	Age	Name	Slaves	Total	Age
Upper Suburbs of New				Jupiton, Manette	2	11	36–55
Orleans—Cont.				Brunette, Betzi	2	11	36–55
Laroque, Ed	2	10	36–55	Romain, P	2	6	24–36
St. Amand, Pierre	17	23	24–36	Emillien, Fred	1	6	36–55
Torrès, Marie	1	7	24–36	Riviere, Celeste	1	10	24–36
Teo., Théodule	1	5	24–36	Chery, Ernest	2	11	36–55
Pouleau, Maurice	5	16	36–55	Jolly, Henriette	5	13	24–36
Sabin, Lolote	5	15	55–100	Benjouin, Charles	3	14	36–55
Spallino, Vallery	3	14	55–100	Sherburne, Maurice	6	10	24–36
Cuvillier, Barth	4	16	36–55	Cinet, Etienne	1	11	36–55
Bertholin, Paul	4	10	36–55	Rousseau, T	6	16	55–100
Brunette, Carmelite	2	10	55–100	Dupuy, Adelaide	10	12	24–36
Rebaudy, Ant	1	9	55–100	Boucher, A. G	6	17	55–100
Bertrand, Rosalie	6	13	55–100	Trevigne, Auguste	5	15	24–36
Populus, Maurice	2	8	55–100	Laignel, Jean	3	11	36–55
Morange, Silvie	3	14	55–100	Brunel, Philip	15	30	55–100
Jolivet, Poupone	5	13	36–55	Courcelle, Mirtille	8	15	36–55
Damien, Alfred	1	11	36–55	Delerry, A	3	12	55–100
Raboul, Ant	2	5	10–24	Boisseau, Manon	8	16	55–100
Macarty, Silvanie	4	13	36–55	Dalon, Auguste	3	10	36–55
Montanno, Albert	3	12	10–24	Donet, Ernest	6	14	36–55
Sacriste, Juliette	9	21	36–55	Snaer, Ambroise	1	7	36–55
Toussaint, Lse	1	5	24–36	Saulet, Jacques	7	17	55–100
Druillet, A	2	10	36–55	Joubert, Mathilde	3	9	55–100
Berger, Théodule	2	12	24–36	Jolly, Ant	3	6	36–55
Montassa, Emille	3	5	36–55	Marie, St. Jean	1	5	36–55
Guéringer, Ernestine	2	9	55–100	Roviaux, Gaston	1	6	24–36
Pioreau, Laurt	13	24	55–100	Beaurpeau, Noël	1	5	36–55
Mauret, Louis	2	8	24–36	Beaurocher, Fredk	5	11	24–36
Carrière, Noël	2	4	36–55	Cheval, Louise P	8	14	55–100
Lacroix, Pierre	1	8	24–36	Cheval, Léandre P	1	8	36–55
Girardy, Wid	4	11	36–55	Abejan, Jos	1	6	36–55
Lébastien, Jean	3	8	24–36	Blanche, Lse. Mia	2	7	36–55
Philistin, Wid	1	10	55–100	Bondellie, Bonne	2	7	24–36
Monnet, Pierre	4	9	24–36	Allegre, Rosiette	1	6	55–100
Despres, Manette	9	20	36–55	Almazor, Mary	3	12	55–100
Henry, Marie R	1	7	55–100	Noël Bel., Ant	3	8	36–55
Renaud, Jacques	4	13	36–55	Bellotte, Pognone	3	10	36–55
Perrin, Rosette	3	14	55–100	Constantin, H	2	4	55–100
Bouny, Marie	4	11	36–55	Dupain, Miss C	1	5	24–36
Gambal, Ant	6	16	36–55	Passement, A. B	2	11	55–100
Legouvée, Marie Lse	1	10	55–100	Poyroux, Miss Ména	2	4	10–24
Barjon (?), D	8	17	55–100	Prieur, Sanite	1	7	36–55
Duvallon, Wid	10	19	55–100	Raphael, Wid	3	4	36–55
Lacoste, Catiche	1	4	24–36	Simon, L	2	7	24–36
Many, Marie	1	5	10–24	Thomassin, B	5	8	55–100
Leroy, Malthilde	1	14	55–100	Pinta, C. B	4	7	24–36
Mayet, Henriette	4	14	36–55	Pilon, Fs	1	7	24–36
Seraphin, Aglaë	1	2	10–24	Baquet, Fs	1	4	24–36
Thiot, Zelie	8	12	36–55	Leroux, Wid	1	8	55–100
Danoranero, D. V	5	17	55–100	Ternien, Miss	1	8	24–36
Boutin, Leon	5	12	24–36	Cornier, L	4	5	24–36
Gautreaux, Geneviève	4	14	36–55	Joublotte, Sanite	2	5	24–36
Noffre, Helene	4	17	55–100	Peyproux, Aug	1	9	55–100
Morcau, Cecile	10	20	36–55	Larien (?), J	9	16	36–55
Conand, Amede	1	4	36–55	Chanal, Martin	2	11	36–55
Durneville, André	2	10	24–36	Belisaire, Severin	5	11	55–100
Lafitte, Siméon	1	9	36–55				

MAINE

Name	Slaves	Total	Age	Name	Slaves	Total	Age
KENNEBEC COUNTY							
Albion							
Tolbut, Abram	1	2	55–100				

MARYLAND

Name	Slaves	Total	Age
ALLEGANY COUNTY			
Peney, Bazle	5	6	55–100
Isaac, Black	1	3	36–55
ANNE ARUNDEL COUNTY			
Barnett, Richard	3	7	36–55
Gambrill, Orang	2	7	55–100
Hoxton, Rd	1	6	24–36
Scosey, Ann	2	6	36–55
Holland, Sophy	2	4	24–36
Johnson, Stephen	1	4	36–55
Harwood of Thos., Richd.	39	42	36–55
Jacobs, Geo	3	7	36–55
Dorsey, Nichs	2	4	24–36
Anderson, Saml	1	3	24–36
Dorsey, Vacheal	1	5	24–36
Meed, M	17	18	100–
Peach, Joseph	1	11	24–36
Wells, George	5	6	10–24
Waters, Wilson	3	4	36–55
Chase, Richard	15	23	55–100
Manidier, Henry	17	25	55–100
Wells, George	5	7	55–100
Barnes, Henry	3	8	36–55
Bryan, Peter	1	8	36–55
Fleetwood, Jane	1	3	24–36
Gray, Ephraim	2	6	24–36
Johnson, Thomas	2	7	36–55
Lee, Charles	2	5	36–55
Leichlightner, Philips	11	16	24–36
Mann, Pero	1	7	55–100
Purdy, Alice	2	3	36–55
Ringgold, Edward	3	4	36–55
Richardson, James	4	5	36–55
Ringgold, Jacob	3	7	36–55
Stephens, Sophia	1	5	36–55
Tunks, John	1	12	55–100
Wilson, Richard	1	8	24–36
Young, Walter	1	2	24–36
Talable, Adam	2	4	55–100
Williams, Abraham	2	3	36–55
Giles, Rachel	1	3	36–55
Dorsey, Jemima	3	4	55–100
Sim, Robert	2	4	24–36
Wells, Daniel	1	4	55–100
Brashears, Gilbert	1	4	24–36
Brown, Joseph	1	2	55–100
Folks, Charity	3	13	55–100
Franklin, York	3	4	36–55
Gantt, Jenny	1	5	55–100
Harris, Thomas	1	5	55–100
Ireland, Mary	5	7	55–100

Name	Slaves	Total	Age
Keys, Moses	1	3	10–24
Lee, Sarah	1	17	36–55
Pully, Jenny	2	3	36–55
Robinson, George	3	4	55–100
Stewart, Ellick	1	3	55–100
City of Annapolis			
Tidd, James	1	3	36–55
Thomas, Rose	1	5	36–55
Williams, Valentine	1	2	55–100
Watkins, Stephen	1	6	36–55
CITY OF BALTIMORE			
First Ward			
Smith, James	1	5	36–55
Sims, Henry	2	3	55–100
Anderson, Saml	3	4	24–36
Barnett, Stephen	1	5	24–36
Thomas, Seth	1	6	24–36
Banks, Benjamin	1	5	55–100
Burk, Thos	1	3	36–55
Second Ward			
Talbot, Benjamin	1	6	36–55
Robinson, Christena	1	4	24–36
Johnston, Nicholas	2	5	36–55
Robinson, Zachariah	1	4	24–36
Buly, Cirus	6	8	36–55
Phillips, Charles	8	9	24–36
Elliott, David	1	6	24–36
Clark, James	1	5	36–55
Cain, Elenor	1	3	55–100
Third Ward			
Wallace, Charles	1	11	55–100
Harden, James	1	3	24–36
Cooper, Thomas	2	5	36–55
Smallwood, Richard	2	7	24–36
Ridgley, Charlotte	1	4	55–100
Fleetwood, Thomas	1	3	36–55
Green, Peter	1	5	36–55
Smith, Rebecca	1	6	24–36
Nelson, Sarah	1	2	36–55
Harriss, Cecelia	1	3	55–100
Cooper, Benjamin	1	3	24–36
Fisher, Levin	3	4	24–36
Smith, Perry	1	3	24–36
Dixson, Perry	1	3	36–55
Fourth Ward			
Williams, Nathaniel	1	8	36–55
Castle, William	1	5	10–24
Grason, Elizabeth	1	7	55–100

MARYLAND—*Continued*

Name	Slaves	Total	Age	Name	Slaves	Total	Age
Fourth Ward—Cont.				Johnson, Job	2	4	36–55
Strupping, Priscilla	1	3	55–100	Parker, Jas	2	7	36–55
Blake, Vincent	1	9	36–55	Tile, Hannah	1	4	55–100
Presco, James	1	8	55–100	Johnson, Richard	1	4	36–55
Hollowday, Ann	1	4	55–100	Carrol, Peter	1	4	55–100
Hollowday, James	2	9	55–100	Smith, Perry	1	6	24–36
				Gamble, Peter	2	5	24–36
Fifth Ward				Wilson, Wm	1	2	24–36
Allen, William	1	3	24–36	Calhoon, Peter	1	3	24–36
Henson, Emory	1	5	24–36	Anderson, James	1	6	55–100
				Howard, James	2	3	24–36
Sixth Ward				Hains, Thomas	1	3	24–36
Lewis, John	5	8	24–36	Mitchel, Ann E	2	3	55–100
				Steward, Stephen	2	3	36–55
Seventh Ward				Fuller, Clm	1	2	36–55
Gage, Dina	1	2	55–100	Primrose, Geo	1	4	36–55
Robinson, Sarah	1	3	36–55				
Ridgely, Loyed	4	5	24–36	*First Collection District*			
Sprigg, Margaret	1	5	36–55	Morris, John B	2	3	55–100
Pinkney, William	1	4	24–36	Smith, Andrew	2	10	24–36
				Hall, Ephraim	1	16	55–100
Ninth Ward				Bishop, John	1	4	55–100
Griffin, Maria	1	8	36–55	Whiper, Luke	1	7	36–55
Sherrick, John F	1	2	55–100	Wallace, Bazil	1	2	55–100
Scott, Margaret	1	2	55–100	Williams, Hannah	1	7	36–55
Thomson, Lewis	1	11	55–100				
Hicks, Emanuel	1	6	55–100	*Second Collection District*			
Butler, Basil	1	6	55–100	Smith, Lindy	1	3	24–36
Clark, Nancy	1	8	24–36	Smith, Joseph	1	3	24–36
Askins, Christ	1	9	36–55	Hooper, Samuel	1	4	55–100
Kill, David	1	4	24–36	Wicks, Jacob	2	11	36–55
West, Charles	5	8	36–55	Saddler, Perry	1	2	36–55
Howard, Edward	1	6	24–36	Jones, Flora	5	6	55–100
Dailey, Richard	1	4	24–36	Hicks, Rosetta	1	2	36–55
Gilles, Ann	1	7	36–55	Bently, Amey	1	5	36–55
Curtis, Henrey	1	9	24–36	Dorsey, Harry	1	4	55–100
Limas, Brudame	1	4	55–100	Brown, Lucy Ann	1	2	55–100
McCay, Robert	1	4	36–55	Preston, Pompey	11	12	24–36
Smith, Edward	1	4	24–36	Brown, Abraham	2	7	36–55
Miller, Henrey	3	6	24–36	Procter, Charlotte	4	6	36–55
Shivers, Widow	1	3	55–100				
Noal, John	1	8	24–36	*Third Collection District*			
Johnston, Charles	4	7	24–36	Jackson, Jeremiah	1	4	36–55
Young, Benj	1	4	36–55	Clark, James	1	7	36–55
Hall, Peter	1	4	36–55				
Ridgeley, Pompey	6	9	36–55	*Fourth Collection District*			
Scott, Charlotte	1	3	24–36	Johnson, Henry	2	3	10–24
Gray, David	3	5	36–55	Carey, John	5	8	36–55
Griffin, Alexander	9	10	55–100	Brooks, Edward	2	5	36–55
Victoire, Mary A	1	3	36–55	Matthews, Alexander	1	3	24–36
Gibson, Jacob	1	4	24–36	Cook, Henry	3	4	36–55
Boston, John	1	2	24–36	Walker, Hannah	4	9	24–36
Bradley, Samuel	3	6	36–55	Brown, G	2	12	36–55
Johnston, Gustus	1	3	24–36	Mickle, Anthony	1	3	10–24
Williams, Dinah	2	8	24–36	Neibours, Elizabeth	6	9	24–36
Johnson, Robert	5	6	24–36	Owings, Sarah	1	4	55–100
Stephens, Littleton	1	6	36–55	Brown, Isaac	1	6	36–55
Snowden, Peter	2	5	24–36	Jackson, Tobias	2	3	24–36

MARYLAND—*Continued*

Name	Slaves	Total	Age	Name	Slaves	Total	Age
Sixth Collection District				Butler, Tom............	1	3	55–100
Govens, Jane (Coled) ...	1	4	55–100	Parker, Jno.............	2	4	24–36
Fenton, James (Coled) ..	1	9	36–55	Gordan, Rebecca........	1	4	36–55
				Thomas, Mikeal........	1	6	24–36
Seventh Collection District				Holler, James...........	1	5	55–100
Patterson, William......	9	10	36–55	Hawkins, James........	2	5	24–36
Price, Robert...........	2	4	10–24	Johnston, Abram.......	1	10	36–55
				Glover, Joseph..........	2	8	36–55
CALVERT COUNTY				Jonas, Spencer..........	1	14	55–100
Hardesty, Samuel.......	3	6	36–55	Share, Moses...........	3	4	36–55
Skinner, Sarah..........	13	16	36–55	Johnston, James........	3	5	55–100
Denton, Susan..........	1	3	100–	Shields, George........	1	5	36–55
Jones, Mathew.........	2	4	24–36	Collins, Henry..........	1	3	24–36
Cooper, Henson........	3	4	24–36	Brown, Robt...........	1	7	24–36
Quill, Benjamin.........	1	4	10–24	Ferl, John.............	1	6	100–
Evans, Sarah...........	1	6	36–55				
				CHARLES COUNTY			
CAROLINE COUNTY				*Durham District*			
Upper District No. 1				Washington, Ignatius....	7	11	36–55
Flamer, William........	2	9	24–36	Greer, James...........	3	5	55–100
Downs, Benjamin.......	1	.4	36–55	Skinner, Clement.......	5	10	36–55
Kennady, David........	2	5	24–36	Queen, Charles.........	2	10	36–55
Fritchett, Samuel.......	2	7	24–36	Butler, Hezekiah........	3	9	24–36
Green, Christopher......	5	6	55–100	Bond, Jane.............	1	2	36–55
Dawson, Saml..........	2	5	24–36	Ray, Abednago.........	1	4	36–55
				Johnson, Samuel........	3	4	36–55
Middle District No. 2				Carnel, Benjamin.......	1	3	55–100
Baynard, Clarricy, Negro	1	5	36–55				
Turner, Aaron, Negro...	2	3	24–36	*Allens Fresh District*			
Clarke, Edward, Negro..	1	3	24–36	Butler, Henry (?).......	1	10	10–24 ?
Boon, Jacob, Negro....	1	3	24–36	Collins, William........	1	5	10–24 ?
Red, Stephen, Negro....	4	5	55–100	Hill, Elizabeth.........	3	5	10–24
Holland, William, Negro.	1	4	10–24	Shurborn, Judy.........	2	4	10–24
Murry, Amy, Negro.....	2	8	36–55	Hall, Betsey...........	1	13	55–100
Sutton, Reason, Negro ..	3	4	24–36	Hungerford, John......	29	30	36–55
Rich, Daniel, Negro....	2	8	36–55	Butler, Charles.........	6	16	24–36
Register, Peter, Negro...	3	6	55–100	Hawkins, Ignatious.....	1	4	55–100
Blake, James, Negro....	2	3	10–24	Smith, William.........	7	8	55–100
Lockerman, Jno.........	1	4	24–36	Dodson, Elizabeth......	1	7	36–55
Green, Levi, Negro......	1	5	24–36	Moore, John...........	7	8	24–36
Rotter, Cidney, Negro...	1	5	36–55	Day, Henry............	3	4	55–100
Hollyday, Richard......	1	2	24–36	Butler, Ignatius.........	2	3	36–55
Jacobs, Mooder, Negro..	1	3	55–100	Procter, Thomas........	1	3	24–36
Hubbard, Daniel, Negro.	4	5	24–36	Morrison, Mary........	1	5	55–100
Bachus, John, Negro....	2	4	55–100				
Willgon, Francis, Negro .	1	4	24–36	DORCHESTER COUNTY			
Chase, Hannah, Negro...	1	4	24–36	*Election District No. 1*			
Stokley, Peter, Negro....	8	9	36–55	Callender, Patrick......	1	4	55–100
Haskins, Edward, Negro.	3	5	55–100	Robinson, Rachel.......	1	2	55–100
Bowdle, Jacob, Negro...	3	5	36–55				
West, Jeremiah, Negro..	2	5	36–55	*Election District No. 2*			
				New Market			
CECIL COUNTY				Cornish, Peter..........	6	8	36–55
First Election District				Chamberlain, Esther....	4	6	36–55
Anderson, Ben..........	1	6	36–55	Hubbard, Peter.........	1	6	36–55
Gans, Clem.............	1	4	24–36	Murray, Prince.........	1	3	24–36
Mercer, George........	1	3	36–55	Washington, John.......	3	7	24–36

MARYLAND—*Continued*

Name	Slaves	Total	Age	Name	Slaves	Total	Age
New Market—Cont.				Cephas, Ibby	3	6	55–100
Dye, Mary	2	3	24–36	Woolford, Nelly	6	7	24–36
Woolford, Adam	1	3	36–55	Young, James, sen	1	3	55–100
Dennis, Casidy	1	9	55–100	Pinder, Stephen	3	6	10–24
Lloyd, Barthenia	3	4	36–55	Cephas, Joseph	1	4	55–100
Smith, Richard	1	4	55–100	Kennard, Nathan	4	5	?
Standley, Jeffrey	2	3	24–36	Smallwood, William	5	7	24–36
Dickerson, Richard	1	7	24–36	Roberts, Edmond	6	7	55–100
Johnson, Abram	1	2	36–55	Scye, Tom	3	4	55–100
Mathews, Diana	1	2	36–55	Quinton, Jacob	1	5	55–100
Warfield, Thomas	4	5	36–55	Johnson of Knot, George	2	7	55–100
Atkinson, Joe	2	4	24–36	Holiday, Thomas	3	6	55–100
Hardcastle, Simon	7	8	36–55	Thompson, Daniel	1	6	24–36
Jenkins, Rosanne	1	3	55–100	Coleman, Daniel	1	5	55–100
Green, Leah	3	7	55–100	Sampson, James	2	7	24–36
Thompson, Jim	6	7	55–100				
Moor, Richard	1	3	24–36	*Election District No. 4*			
Thompson, Eliza	4	5	55–100	Travers, Thomas	3	4	55–100
Smallwood, Ezekiel	5	6	55–100	Gainby, Jacob	3	7	24–36
Kier, Joshua	4	5	36–55	Stanley, James	1	3	36–55
Dockins, Peter	4	5	36–55	Ellis, Thomas	3	6	36–55
Henry, Mahala	1	3	10–24	Saunders, Rose	1	3	10–24
Banks, William	1	4	55–100	Dickson, Jacob	5	9	55–100
Coleman, George	3	4	24–36	Keene, Phebe	3	4	24–36
Cornish, Joshua	1	7	36–55	Woodland, Cilas	1	3	36–55
Darby, John	1	4	55–100	Manokin, Charles	2	10	36–55
Johnson, William	1	2	55–100	Bright, Fountain	3	6	24–36
Horsman, Eliza	1	6	36–55	Keene, Draper	1	8	36–55
Dillen, Lucy	1	4	36–55	Slater, Robert	2	4	55–100
Beard, Charles	3	6	36–55	Colson, Drew	1	3	55–100
Standley, Robert	1	8	55–100	Thomas, Elizabeth	3	9	24–36
Young, Adam	3	5	36–55	Henry, James	1	2	24–36
Neal, Thomas	1	2	100–	Keene, Lydia	2	9	55–100
Sullivan, Minty	2	4	55–100	Bright, Moses	1	7	24–36
Parker, George	4	6	36–55	Travers, Francis	1	11	36–55
Pearce, Nancy	4	5	55–100	Barnes, Henry	1	3	36–55
Hall, Joseph	1	5	55–100	Brohawn, Rhoda	1	11	36–55
Nace, Jesse	2	4	24–36	Cornish, Any	1	6	24–36
Smart, Richard	1	3	55–100	Pattison, Samuel	5	10	36–55
Fisher, Isaac	1	5	24–36	Willson, Jacob	5	6	36–55
Pharrow, Sarah	1	2	24–36	Edwards, Charles	2	7	55–100
Mitchell, Ralph	7	8	36–55	Travers, Dinah	1	7	36–55
Brooks, Dennis	1	6	55–100				
Cephas, Sophia	1	5	36–55	*Election District No. 5*			
Tilghman, James	1	4	36–55	Dier, Margaret	5	7	36–55
Woolford, Jeffrey	1	6	55–100				
Waters, John	4	6	24–36	*Election District No. 6*			
Lee, Harry	1	11	55–100	Ross, Henry	3	6	36–55
Crier, James	1	6	36–55				
Jolly, David	1	4	24–36	*Election District No. 7*			
Atkinson, Tom	4	12	36–55	Addison, Jacob	6	7	36–55
Parker, Isaac	1	2	36–55	Woolford, Ezekiel	1	3	55–100
Knotter, Hewit	1	2	36–55				
Camper, Charles	1	3	55–100	*Election District No. 8*			
Nicols, James	2	10	36–55	Brooks, Curtis	2	6	24–36
Banup, Ansy	5	6	24–36	Macer, Jacob	3	4	36–55
Lockerman, Prissa	1	2	36–55	Pendleton, Lovey	1	5	36–55

MARYLAND—*Continued*

Name	Slaves	Total	Age	Name	Slaves	Total	Age
Elec. Dist. No. 8—Cont.				*District No. 2*			
Bennet, Manuel	2	15	36–55	*Frederick Town*			
Lee, David	1	3	36–55	Hillman, Aaron	1	3	36–55
Bird, Toby	5	7	36–55	Mitchell, Casandra	2	4	24–36
Blake, Nancy	7	9	36–55	Boone, David	3	6	55–100
Quash, Alsy	3	6	55–100	Hawkins, Aaron	2	3	55–100
Johns, Sarah	3	4	55–100	Gaines, William	2	3	24–36
Smith, Allen	4	8	55–100	Gray, Joseph	1	2	36–55
Brown, John	1	12	55–100	Harper, Alley	1	3	24–36
Macer, Henry	5	6	55–100	Hammond, Samuel	1	7	36–55
Lee, Levin	3	10	55–100	Pratt, Solomon	2	7	55–100
Lee, Nero	1	3	55–100	Carr, Isaac	1	7	55–100
Nutter, Nancy	1	3	24–36	Gordon, Thomas	1	4	36–55
Johnson, Charles	2	4	36–55	Dorsey, Harriet	1	4	36–55
Hooper, John	1	9	55–100	Davis, Francis	2	3	24–36
Green, Allen	9	10	36–55	Schneevilly, Edward	8	12	36–55
Ross, Priscilla	8	9	36–55	Devan, William	1	4	10–24
Cook, Robert	1	8	36–55	Hill, Anthony	1	2	55–100
Nicols, Moses	3	6	36–55	Leake, Peter	1	5	55–100
Stanley, Nathan	3	4	36–55	Roberson, Esther	2	3	55–100
Nunum, John	6	9	36–55	Noland, Elisabeth	1	5	24–36
Kennedy, Jeremiah	1	3	10–24				
Stanley, Charles	2	4	10–24	*District No. 4*			
Blake, James	4	12	36–55	Groce, Sampson	1	2	55–100
Cromwell, Shadrack	2	9	24–36				
Bruffit, Aaron	4	5	55–100	*Lewiston*			
Griffith, Sophia	1	5	24–36	McKinney, Patsy	2	8	55–100
Barnes, Scippio	2	7	55–100				
				District No. 8			
FREDERICK COUNTY				*Woodsboro*			
District No. 1				Wicks, Jane	1	3	55–100
Green, Ceaser	2	7	55–100	Key, Sarah	1	5	24–36
Ingland, Arch	1	4	24–36	Murdok, Aaron	1	6	24–36
Rollings, Henry	1	6	24–36	Roberts, Mary	3	7	55–100
Caleb, Joseph	1	8	36–55	Todd, Upton	2	3	24–36
Waters, Jacob	2	3	55–100	Jackson, John	1	3	36–55
Duffin, Bassil	2	4	10–24				
Berrit, William	1	5	36–55	*Uniontown*			
Combs, Jenne	1	3	36–55	Moales, Lloyd	1	2	36–55
Norriss, Thos	2	8	24–36	Stoner, John, Jnr	2	13	24–36
Ford, Nathan	1	8	10–24				
Dawkins, Henry	1	2	36–55	HARFORD COUNTY			
Armstrong, John	1	7	55–100	Hipkins, Charles G	2	6	36–55
Carroll, Polly	3	6	36–55	Carlile, Washington	3	7	36–55
Rollings, Mary	1	4	24–36	More, Samuel	3	5	36–55
				Hendley, John D	8	9	36–55
District No. 9				Smith, Samuel W	6	12	10–24
Stuart, Nathan	1	9	36–55	Hall, William B	17	22	36–55
Proctor, Michael	1	8	36–55	Banks, James	5	6	36–55
Coats, George	2	3	55–100	Amos, Henry	1	3	55–100
Thorn, Frederick	1	6	24–36	Scott, Susan	1	2	36–55
Davis, Eli	2	5	36–55	Amos, Thomas	4	5	55–100
Valentine, Amos	3	5	36–55	Witmore, Abraham	1	8	36–55
Ogle, Samuel	1	5	24–36				
				KENT COUNTY			
District No. 3				Ward, Letty	3	4	55–100
Caywood, Abraham	1	6	36–55	Anderson, John B. H	6	7	10–24

MARYLAND—*Continued*

Name	Slaves	Total	Age	Name	Slaves	Total	Age
KENT COUNTY—*Cont.*				TALBOT COUNTY			
Byram, Edward	1	2	55–100	Scott, Philomon	1	3	36–55
Tilghman, Susan	3	4	36–55	Dorrell, Wm	5	7	24–36
Nicols, Moses	1	3	55–100	Tilghman, Ann	6	11	55–100
Fountain, Joe	1	6	36–55	Cornish, Tilly	2	6	36–55
Bordley, Lisbon	2	4	55–100	Stokely, Ezekiel	1	3	36–55
Warner, Harry	3	7	36–55	Kelly, Joseph	4	5	100–
Warren, David	1	3	55–100	Hall, Ara (?)	2	4	24–36
Wickes, Peter	2	10	55–100	Banning, Jerry	2	6	100–
Hollyday, William	6	7	36–55	Tripp, Dick	4	11	24–36
Cuff, Thomas	3	6	55–100	Dove, James	2	3	55–100
Rogers, Eliza	1	4	24–36	Mackey, Susan	1	3	36–55
Boyer, Lucy	10	16	36–55	Tripp, Bill	1	5	36–55
Boyer, Philip	2	5	36–55	Potter, Grace	1	11	55–100
Hynson, Joseph	1	6	36–55	Goldsborough, Jane	2	5	100–
Forman, Ezekiel	1	3	24–36	Sinclair, Joe	3	4	24–36
Woodland, Emory	3	4	10–24	Hawkins, Tom	1	2	55–100
Thomas, Moses	1	4	10–24	Nelson, Parris	1	7	36–55
Anderson, Henry	1	11	55–100	Thomas, James	1	2	36–55
Richardson, Moses	1	6	55–100	Brown, Sarah	1	3	55–100
Leger, Philis	2	5	55–100	Hopkins, Violett	3	6	24–36
Jones, James	1	4	24–36	Calloway, Philip	1	6	55–100
Pearce, Maria	1	4	55–100	Madden, Crecy	2	5	36–55
Rogers, Samuel	2	5	55–100	Brion, Aron	3	6	55–100
Smith, Elijah	4	5	24–36	Williams, Isaac	1	4	24–36
Mechanick, James	1	7	24–36	Potter, Nero	3	4	36–55
Constable, John	13	14	10–24	Pipes, Peter	1	5	55–100
Palmer, Priscilla	1	6	36–55	Bantom, Joe	1	3	55–100
Hynson, Charles	2	7	36–55	Cuff, Horris	5	6	24–36
Anderson, Thomas	3	4	36–55	Jone (June ?)	1	2	36–55
Philips, George	1	7	24–36	Tender, Dembey	3	7	24–36
Taylor, Stepney	1	3	36–55	Warner, Cain	1	2	24–36
Rasin, William	1	6	36–55	Donsbuary, Scipio	2	3	24–36
Lamb, Rachel	1	5	55–100	Tillison, Henry	1	2	24–36
Massey, James Taes (?)	1	3	36–55	Summers, Henry	1	4	55–100
Dudley, Perigrine	6	7	36–55	Porter, John	4	5	24–36
Simmons, Stephen	1	4	36–55	Harriss, James	2	3	55–100
Mason, Isaac	2	5	36–55	Cox, Jenny	1	6	100–
Anderson, Richard	5	6	55–100	Hill, Sarah Fox	4	5	36–55
Mason, William	1	7	36–55	Mackey, Ross	2	5	36–55
Mann, Abraham	2	7	55–100	Caulk, James	3	5	36–55
Chambers, William	1	6	55–100	Banning, Ned	2	5	36–55
Graves, Milky	1	3	24–36	Bantom, Henry	7	8	36–55
Black, Jacob	1	5	55–100	Benson, Solomon	4	13	10–24
Harding, Stephen	2	8	36–55	Homes, Henry	4	6	24–36
Wilson, William	1	2	55–100	Murry, Samuel	4	5	36–55
Doman, Daniel, Jr.	2	9	24–36	Harriss, Leven	4	5	36–55
Jones, Thomas	1	2	55–100	Bantom, Lilly	2	5	36–55
Hollingsworth, Benjamin	4	5	55–100	Mobry, Jacob	3	5	10–24
Bassle, William	7	8	24–36	Brooks, George	3	6	36–55
Harris, Jacob	4	10	55–100	Cuff, Sally	2	3	55–100
Moffett, Samuel	2	5	55–100	Brooks, George	5	6	36–55
Hackett, Clem	2	4	36–55	Downes, Edward	5	7	36–55
Wilson, William	2	3	55–100	Brooks, David	7	8	55–100
Williams, Sarah	1	2	55–100	Clash, Wrighton	1	2	?
Grey, Susan	1	3	24–36	Thomas, Thomas	3	4	24–36
Wilson, Trump	1	2	36–55	Williams, Charles	1	5	10–24

MARYLAND—*Continued*

Name	Slaves	Total	Age	Name	Slaves	Total	Age
TALBOT COUNTY—*Cont.*				Sturges, William	1	10	55–100
King, Daniel	2	6	36–55	Purnell, Nimrod	5	11	36–55
Barrott, Samuel	2	4	55–100	Turpin, Elijah	4	5	55–100
Commons, Stephen	1	3	10–24	Robins, Rhoda	1	5	36–55
Nicols, Philip	2	10	24–36	Messick, Draper	2	3	55–100
Burley, Richard	2	6	36–55	Townsend, Sophia	4	5	55–100
				Stevenson, Arthur	1	4	55–100
WASHINGTON COUNTY				Collins, Levin	1	2	24–36
Long, Catherine	4	7	55–100	Hammond, Jacob	3	5	55–100
Rideout, Charles	3	7	24–36	Hammond, Isaac	3	8	55–100
Harris, Jno.	1	5	24–36	Norris, Hessy	1	8	55–100
Howard, Lewis	1	6	36–55	Purnell, Josiah	3	4	36–55
Negro Phil	1	3	36–55	Morris, Minty	1	9	10–24
Cranford, James	3	6	24–36	Purnell, Amos	1	3	55–100
McHenry Neg (Negro?)	2	4	36–55	Bowen, William	1	4	36–55
				Marshall, Caleb	6	11	36–55
WORCESTER COUNTY				Miller, Ann	5	7	36–55
Mills, Robert	1	9	36–55	Rackliffe, Draper	1	6	55–100
Parks, Henry	1	2	55–100	Stevenson, Jacob	2	4	55–100
Dennis, Rose	8	10	55–100	Johnson, Peter	3	4	36–55
Riggin, Joseph	3	6	36–55	Massy, Hannah	1	2	36–55
Long, Lydia	2	4	55–100	Rockliffe, Jesse	2	3	55–100
Layfield, Henry	1	8	36–55	Brevard, Isaac	4	5	24–36
Bayly, York	5	7	24–36	Massy, Peter	1	5	24–36
Long, Stephen	1	7	36–55	Pitts, Lydia	1	2	55–100
Mills, James	1	7	36–55	Gray, Luke	7	9	55–100
Purnell, Levin	1	5	36–55	Holland, Sarah	1	4	24–36
Tarpin, Titus	5	6	55–100	Pitts, Milby	1	3	55–100
Ross, Robert	1	4	10–24	Selby, James	1	3	55–100
White, Jasper	1	6	36–55	Whittington, Ephraim	2	3	36–55
Jenkins, Isaac	1	5	55–100	Handy, Richard	1	5	36–55
Purnell, Minadab	5	7	36–55	Johnson, Daniel	1	3	36–55
Purnell, Lucretia	2	4	36–55	Johnson, Rachel	2	4	55–100
Purnell, Peter	8	10	55–100	Dashiell, Jacob	1	6	36–55
Purnell, Sacker	5	8	36–55	Sturges, Jessee	3	4	55–100
Purnell, Peter	8	9	24–36	Fookes, Easther	2	5	36–55

MISSISSIPPI

Name	Slaves	Total	Age	Name	Slaves	Total	Age
ADAMS COUNTY				Martin, Samuel	1	7	36–55
Winn, George	16	17	55–100	Simpson, Gloster	2	5	36–55
				Harris, Hardy	1	6	55–100
City of Natchez				Holly, Christopher	3	5	55–100
Carey, Robert M.	2	4	10–24	Moore, David	5	6	24–36
Miller, Jas.	5	12	24–36				
Battles, Harriet	1	3	24–36	HANCOCK COUNTY			
Gilson, Sam	5	6	10–24	Asmard, Charles, Senior	3	4	100–
				Benoit, Benard, Senior	6	8	55–100
CLAIBORNE COUNTY				Perkins, William P.	17	18	10–24
Willis, Mary	1	5	36–55	WARREN COUNTY			
Bell, Henry	4	5	55–100	Miller, Elisha	1	3	24–36
Butler, Hanibal	1	5	36–55				

MISSOURI

Name	Slaves	Total	Age	Name	Slaves	Total	Age
FRANKLIN COUNTY				ST. CHARLES COUNTY			
Rogers, Lewis	1	8	36–55	Buet, Louise	1	7	36–55

MISSOURI—*Continued*

Name	Slaves	Total	Age	Name	Slaves	Total	Age
PERRY COUNTY				**NEW MADRID COUNTY**			
Dickson, Joseph	3	4	36–55	Scarret, Sally	1	1	36–55

NEW HAMPSHIRE

Name	Slaves	Total	Age	Name	Slaves	Total	Age
ROCKINGHAM COUNTY				Cutler, Rufus	1	5	55–100
Portsmouth				Cutler, Rufus T.	1	5	24–36
Whipple, Joshua	1	2	24–36				

NEW JERSEY

Name	Slaves	Total	Age	Name	Slaves	Total	Age
BERGEN COUNTY				**MONMOUTH COUNTY**			
Pompton Township				*Middletown*			
Green, Sizar	1	7	24–36	Holmes, Hercules	1	3	36–55
				Holmes, Isaac	1	4	36–55
ESSEX COUNTY							
Elizabeth Township				*Frechold*			
Stout, Silas	2	8	24–36	Wolley, Nean	3	5	24–36
Van Horn, Richard	1	4	24–36				
Dunn, John	1	3	36–55	**MORRIS COUNTY**			
Messalier, Henry	1	6	24–36	*Township of Morris*			
				Cutler, Jacob	2	4	36–55
Township of Acquackononk				*Jefferson Township*			
Sip, Thomas	1	2	36–55	*Chatham*			
				Linn, Cato	1	3	36–55
BURLINGTON COUNTY				**HUNTERDON COUNTY**			
Township of Nottingham				*Trenton*			
Morris, Thomas	2	5	24–36	Hulicks, Jas	1	3	36–55
				Hutchins, Perry	2	3	36–55
Township of Springfield				*Laurence*			
Bowan, Robert	1	3	24–36	Duncan, Phillis	1	4	24–36

NEW YORK

Name	Slaves	Total	Age	Name	Slaves	Total	Age
MONTGOMERY COUNTY				*Thompson Street*			
Minden				Jones, John	2	5	55–100
Wilson, Thomas	3	4	24–36	Walker, Benjamin	1	2	24–36
Jackson, Abraham	1	2	10–24	Scott, John	3	6	55–100
				Kip, Sara	1	2	24–36
Canajoharie Village				Thomas, Charles	4	7	24–36
Cockburn, Elizabeth	1	2	10–24	Oatfield, Andrew	4	6	10–24
Hawn, William	1	4	36–55	Low, Abraham	1	3	36–55
Livingston, Dian	2	6	55–100				
Lando, Henry	4	5	24–36	**PUTNAM COUNTY**			
Clady, Robert	3	5	24–36	*Patterson*			
Day, William	3	4	36–55	Townsend, Joseph	2	3	55–100
				TIOGA COUNTY			
Florida				*Catharine*			
Freeman, Joseph	1	3	24–36	Rice, Tobias, Col.	1	2	10–24
				Hall, James, Col.	1	3	10–24
NEW YORK CITY				**WASHINGTON COUNTY**			
King Street				*Cambridge*			
Ritchinson, William	1	2	10–24	Hoase, Sunn	1	3	55–100

NORTH CAROLINA

Name	Slaves	Total	Age	Name	Slaves	Total	Age
ANSON COUNTY				Hornablow, Marey......	2	6	36–55
Jones, Thomas.........	3	12	36–55	Iredell, Jeffrey.......	1	7	100–
				How, Lucey...........	3	4	55–100
BEAUFORT COUNTY				Littlejohn, John........	1	4	24–36
Washington				Johnson, Gustavus A.....	4	12	36–55
Anderson, Hull (?)......	4	8	36–55	Bozman, James........	1	2	36–55
Bonner, Jos.............	2	3	36–55				
Brown, Edme..........	1	2	36–55	**CRAVEN COUNTY**			
Walker, Betsy.........	3	7	10–24	Stanly, James G........	10	11	55–100
Moore, Church.........	2	4	24–36	Green, James Y.........	4	8	36–55
Brown, John...........	2	4	36–55	Hollister, Thomas.......	1	7	36–55
Newton, Clarrissa.......	4	9	24–36	Street, Delia...........	2	3	55–100
Allen, Abram M........	1	7	24–36				
Moore, Eli.............	3	7	24–36	*Town of Newbern*			
Rose, Easter (?)........	1	3	36–55	Mumford, Donum......	10	27	55–100
				Austin, Anne...........	1	2	36–55
North Creek Town				Warrick, Brister........	8	9	36–55
Walker, Thos..........	2	4	55–100	Green, John R..........	6	10	36–55
Bowen, Thos..........	2	4	36–55	Lisbon, Matilda........	2	4	10–24
				Warrick, Brister........	1	6	55–100
BERTIE COUNTY				Garrett, Jane...........	1	4	55–100
James, Mary...........	1	3	36–55	Stanly, John S..........	18	22	24–36
James, Sally...........	1	2	36–55	Stanly, John C..........	14	26	55–100
Hill, Penelope.........	3	6	55–100				
Ash, Jane..............	5	6	55–100	**CUMBERLAND COUNTY**			
Tutle, Willie..........	1	2	55–100	*(The Division West Side*			
				Cape Fear)			
BLADEN COUNTY				*Bones Creek Dist.*			
Bowen, Gooden E.......	44	45	36–55	MacIver, Wining (?)....	1	5	36–55
Spendlove, Eliza........	1	6	36–55	Jackson, Polly..........	1	2	36–55
Spendlove, Molsy.......	3	5	24–36				
Blanks, Michael........	1	2	24–36	*East Side of Cape Fear*			
Allen, Samuel..........	4	5	24–36	Hadley, Bella...........	1	2	55–100
Spendlove, Ann........	1	9	24–36	Artis, Lucretia..........	1	2	36–55
Smith, Catharine......	1	11	24–36	Tutte (Tutle), William ..	1	4	55–100
				Jordan, Judy..........	1	2	55–100
BRUNSWICK COUNTY				Alvis, Esther...........	3	4	36–55
Potter, John A..........	4	8	24–36	Munroe, Daniel........	1	2	10–24
McKenzie, Jimboy (?)..	2	4	55–100	Wood, John............	4	8	24–36
				Freeman, Sally........	1	2	10–24
CAMDEN COUNTY							
Griffin, Samuel........	1	5	100–	*Town of Fayetteville*			
Spelmon, Thomas......	4	5	24–36	Grimes, Thomas........	1	4	36–55
Spelmon, Owen........	2	5	36–55	Hammonds, Elsey.......	5	9	55–100
				Dennis, Phillis..........	4	5	36–55
CASWELL COUNTY				Revels, Margaret......	2	9	55–100
Day, Thomas..........	2	6	24–36	Mallett, Betty..........	1	5	36–55
Jones, Mary...........	1	2	24–36	Dunn, James...........	3	4	36–55
Wilson, John (Free Col'd)	4	11	24–36	Ragland, George W......	1	7	36–55
Caswell, Allen..........	3	4	36–55	Mallett, Charles........	36	37	10–24
Worsham, James........	1	4	55–100	Chester, Lott...........	2	7	24–36
CHATHAM COUNTY				**DAVIDSON COUNTY**			
Town of Pittsboro				Hatcher, Tabitha.......	1	5	55–100
Anderson, Jerry.........	1	3	55–100	Cain, Jesse.............	1	5	24–36
				David, Sarah...........	1	3	36–55
CHOWAN COUNTY							
Town of Edenton							
Grean, Ritchard M......	4	8	24–36				

NORTH CAROLINA—*Continued*

Name	Slaves	Total	Age	Name	Slaves	Total	Age
EDGECOMB COUNTY				Jones, Pompey.........	2	3	55–100
District No. 1				Hammons, Olive........	1	7	36–55
Tarborough							
Scott, Elizabeth........	3	4	24–36	HERTFORD COUNTY			
Thompson, William.....	5	6	24–36	Melton, Meede.........	2	8	55–100
				Mandley, Penelope......	1	7	36–55
District No. 15				Renalds, Jeston.........	2	3	24–36
Morgan, Henry.........	1	5	24–36	Jordan, Lewis..........	3	4	10–24
				Roberts, David.........	2	6	36–55
FRANKLIN COUNTY				Renalds, Jeston.........	1	3	24–36
Louisburg—Perrie's Dist.				Boon, David...........	1	5	55–100
Armstrong, John........	1	2	36–55				
Williams, Jeremiah......	3	4	24–36	LENOIR COUNTY			
				Dutton, Nellie..........	1	3	55–100
Pearce's Dist.							
Tucker, Robert.........	2	6	36–55	MARTIN COUNTY			
				Crichlon, John..........	24	25	36–55
Bledsoe's Dist.				James, Larry..........	1	5	24–36
Charles, Thomas'es......	6	7	36–55	James, Martha.........	1	3	55–100
Foster's Dist.				NASH COUNTY			
Mitchel, John..........	3	6	36–55	Revill, Humphrey.......	14	18	36–55
Edward's Dist.				NORTHAMPTON COUNTY			
Blacknel, Thomas.......	7	15	36–55	Wheeler, Anthony......	2	3	36–55
Hicks, Benjamin........	4	5	24–36	Boone, Ruthy..........	1	2	55–100
Alford's Dist.				NEW HANOVER COUNTY			
Mitchel, Milbry........	2	6	36–55	Ware, George..........	1	8	36–55
				Mosely, Wanely (?).....	1	6	36–55
Dunn's Dist.				Cruise (?), Mary........	3	8	36–55
Evans, Rosetta.........	2	7	24–36	Larington, Simon.......	1	1	36–55
				Bazadeir, Phillis........	1	5	36–55
GATES COUNTY				Buffo, William..........	1	2	10–24
Martin, Jottro (?).......	1	6	36–55	Pajay, Lewis...........	4	5	10–24
Cuff, Nisom............	1	2	36–55	Walker, John...........	44	45	36–55
Hansford, Thomas......	1	4	55–100	Hazell, Roger..........	5	9	10–24
				Campbell, James........	2	4	24–36
GRANVILLE COUNTY				Sampson, Henry	5	9	36–55
(North Regiment)							
Fain, Jacob............	1	8	55–100	ONSLOW COUNTY			
Cousins, Nelson........	1	8	36–55	Loomiss, Caesar........	2	3	55–100
				Jarmen, Benjamin......	5	7	55–100
HALIFAX COUNTY				Tatom, Sally..........	1	12	36–55
Jourdan, John..........	1	6	24–36	ORANGE COUNTY			
Richardson, Absalom....	1	11	36–55	*(North Dist.)*			
				Hartgrove, Fed.........	3	4	36–55
District of North Carolina				Peters, Lucy...........	1	2	55–100
2nd Regiment District							
Howard, Miles.........	2	9	24–36	PASQUOTANK COUNTY			
Jones, Tabitha.........	1	2	24–36	Morris, Will., Senr. (of			
Mills, Wesley...........	2	3	24–36	Colr.................	2	10	10–24
Worrel, Lucy...........	1	3	10–24	Price, Aaron (of Colr.)...	1	13	24–36
Taylor, Sally..........	1	4	55–100	Harvey, Alfred (of Colr.)	1	2	24–36
Johnson, Amy..........	3	5	24–36				
Taylor, Peggy..........	1	9	55–100	PERQUIMANS			
Cain, Malissa..........	1	3	24–36	Bogue, Dorothy (of Colr.)	1	5	36–55
Curtis, Ann............	3	8	36–55				

NORTH CAROLINA—*Continued*

Name	Slaves	Total	Age	Name	Slaves	Total	Age
PERQUIMANS—*Cont.*				WAKE COUNTY			
Randol, Charlotte (of Colr.)	1	9	36–55	Jones, Allen	6	10	24–36
				Burwell, Pope	1	2	36–55
Winslow, Mills (of Colr.)	7	8	36–55	Jones, Charles	3	4	55–100
Robins, Jacobs (of Colr.)	1	6	36–55	Malon, John (Colored)	3	5	36–55
Overton, Judith (of Colr.)	1	3	10–24	Green, Samuel	7	10	36–55
Nixon, Charlotte (of Colr.)	2	3	55–100	Scott, John D	4	6	55–100
Wadkins, James (of Colr.)	4	6	55–100	*St. Maries District*			
Wadkins, Nathaniel (of Colr.)	4	5	36–55	Wilson, Marsh	1	3	24–36
Overton, Winney (of Colr.)	1	4	36–55	Simms, Nancy	1	2	100–
				Evins, Abigail	4	8	10–24
Modlin, Nancy (of Colr.)	1	6	55–100	Smith, William	2	7	10–24
Overton, Penny (of Colr.)	2	5	36–55	Dunn, John	5	6	10–24
Overton, Levina (of Colr.)	1	5	24–36	Snellings, Silvans	2	21	36–55
Overton, Theny (of Colr.)	1	5	10–24	Taylor, Prudy	1	2	36–55
Overton, Nelly (of Colr.)	1	3	10–24	Holmes, William	3	8	36–55
Winslow, Rose (of Colr.)	3	4	55–100	Seawell, Phil	5	6	36–55
White, Luke (of Colr.)	5	6	36–55	Woodward, Sally	1	2	24–36
Lawrence, Sampson (of Colr.)	7	9	55–100	Maxwell, Polly	4	11	24–36
				WARREN COUNTY			
PITT COUNTY				Cosey, William	1	8	55–100
Brown, Med	3	4	24–36	Day, John	1	3	55–100
				Holmes, Stephen	1	4	55–100
RICHMOND COUNTY				Burt, Jacob	1	5	55–100
Mask, Pleasant M	8	9	10–24	Evans, Isaac	1	7	24–36
				Evans, Tabby	1	6	55–100
ROBESON COUNTY				Evans, Matthew	5	7	55–100
Lowrie, James	5	14	55–100	Green, Thomas	1	7	55–100
				WASHINGTON COUNTY			
SAMPSON COUNTY				Boston, Nancy	1	3	55–100
Pope, West	1	8	10–24	WAYNE COUNTY			
				Burnet, Joel	3	7	24–36
STOKES COUNTY				WILKES COUNTY			
Shepperd, William	1	5	55–100	Anthony, Negro	1	4	36–55
Mason, Ralph	1	3	55–100				

OHIO

Name	Slaves	Total	Age	Name	Slaves	Total	Age
WARREN COUNTY							
Wayne Township							
Ferguson, Charles, Col	6	9	24–36				

PENNSYLVANIA

Name	Slaves	Total	Age	Name	Slaves	Total	Age
ALLEGHENY COUNTY				Cary, William	2	6	36–55
Borough of Allegheny Town				Lewis, Gideon	3	6	36–55
				Merrit, Prince	4	5	10–24
Jackson, Powell	1	2	24–36	Riley, Jacob	5	6	10–24
				Campbell, Samuel	3	5	24–36
BUCKS COUNTY				Campbell, Jesse	1	3	10–24
Paxson, Jos.	2	6	24–36				
Lambert, William	4	7	24–36	CHESTER COUNTY			
Moort, Jane	3	5	24–36	*East Nottingham Township*			
Barry, Robert	3	6	24–36	Green, Stacey	3	5	55–100
Harris, Robert	3	6	24–36				
Brown, Peter	2	6	100–				

PENNSYLVANIA—*Continued*

Name	Slaves	Total	Age	Nome	Slaves	Total	Age
Delaware County				*Philadelphia*			
Aston				Gallaway, Isaac........	1	3	10–24
Gibson, Charles........	1	6	24–36				
				York County			
Franklin County				*York Borough*			
Montgomery Township				Goodridge, William.....	1	9	10–24
Maxwell, William.......	1	5	10–24	Hartman, Charles......	2	5	55–100
Cuff, Sampson.........	1	7	24–36				
Blackburn, John.......	1	5	24–36	*Spring Garden Township*			
				Johnston, John.........	1	5	10–24
Lancaster County							
Conestoga Township							
Robison, Solomon......	2	6	55–100				

RHODE ISLAND

Providence				Ray, John.............	1	3	55–100
Treadwell, Philip.......	1	5	10–24	Hamlin, Wyllys........	1	2	24–36

SOUTH CAROLINA

Name	Slaves	Total	Age	Nome	Slaves	Total	Age
Abbeville County				*Christ Church*			
Davis, Ezekiel.........	1	3	36–55	Legare, John D.........	12	17	?
Payne, Jerry...........	2	3	24–36	Venning, Robert........	30	32	10–24
				Venning, Nicholas, Junr..	7	9	24–36
Beaufort County							
Brown, Alexander.......	15	17	55–100	**St. James Santee**			
Houston, Ann..........	1	9	36–55	Aiken, Thomas.........	7	15	55–100
St. Luke's Parish				*City of Charleston*			
Bing, Gordon..........	1	8	24–36	*Ward No. 1*			
Cuthbert, Sarah........	3	4	55–100	Parsons, Emmey........	2	5	24–36
				Veree, Christiana.......	1	4	24–36
St. Peter's Parish				James, Henry..........	4	7	24–36
Powers, Mack..........	1	3	36–55	Cain, John.............	6	14	55–100
				Spencer, Amey.........	1	5	24–36
Berkeley				Wilkinson, Scipio.......	2	10	100–
St. John's				Duncan, Rebecca.......	3	17	24–36
Eady, Daniel..........	7	8	100–	Leach (Seach?), Sarah...	7	29	36–55
				Fell, Eleanor...........	3	6	24–36
St. Stephen's				Walker, Samuel.........	24	25	36–55
Blute, Hester..........	1	5	55–100	Ward, Fortune.........	8	9	36–55
Davis, Samuel..........	1	4	55–100	Best, Amaretta.........	12	13	10–24
Freeman, Jacob........	4	8	55–100	Holman, Susan.........	1	8	24–36
Wilson, Jenny..........	16	21	55–100	Huger, Sarah...........	1	3	55–100
				Vanderhorst, Ebenezer..	1	2	10–24
St. Thomas & St. Dennis				Morrison, Pollidore......	14	15	24–36
Collins, Robert.........	11	20	55–100	Brown, Moses..........	2	4	10–24
Collins, Jonathan.......	3	6	55–100	Mitchell, Jane.........	15	25	24–36
Collins, William........	1	4	24–36	See, Edward............	2	12	24–36
Capers, Thomas F.......	47	48	36–55	Mitchell, Abigail........	1	6	55–100
Cumbo, Susan..........	6	9	36–55	Ricard, Sally..........	1	2	24–36
Fowler, Stanhope.......	5	13	36–55	Inglis, Eleanor.........	1	5	10–24
Givins, Abraham.......	1	3	55–100	Gardner, Jack..........	4	8	36–55
Smith, Robert..........	8	9	55–100	Wilson, George.........	3	9	24–36
Waring, Daniel J........	41	42	55–100	Prereze, François.......	6	7	24–36
Warren, Juba..........	8	9	55–100	Rogers, Mary..........	1	5	55–100
				Monies, Jane..........	1	6	36–55

SOUTH CAROLINA—*Continued*

Name	Slaves	Total	Age	Name	Slaves	Total	Age
Ward No. 2				Creighton, Grace	8	14	36–55
Ingles, Thomas	11	17	36–55	Roteraux, Mary Ann	1	2	10–24
Douglass, Margaret	7	8	24–36	Fenwick, Mary	11	14	10–24
Cotton, Eleanor	12	13	24–36	Harper, Jack	3	4	55–100
Bush, Adam	7	9	36–55	Ferguson, Sarah	8	9	55–100
Chisolm, William	1	6	10–24	Pere, Emele	8	11	24–36
Sommers, Rosetta	3	4	24–36	Mills, Sally	5	10	24–36
Elliott, Daphne	2	3	24–36	Wilson, Dolly	5	6	55–100
Holmes, Sarah	12	17	24–36	Allen, Martha	12	13	24–36
Brown, Peter	3	12	24–36	Martin, Elizabeth	8	10	55–100
Savage, Silvey	4	14	55–100	Crawley, Frank	13	15	55–100
Lloyd, Dina	6	10	24–36	White, Betsy	1	2	24–36
Sorie, François	1	4	10–24	Lindsay, Eliza	2	3	10–24
Brown, John	3	6	24–36	Evans, Charlotte	3	6	10–24
May, Ann	3	8	24–36	Bremar, Rebecca	3	8	10–24
Cooper, William	2	10	36–55	Cooper, Cecelia	3	6	24–36
Keeter, Mary	6	7	10–24	Simmons, Affey	6	7	10–24
Graves, Mindas (?)	5	6	24–36	Cochran, Eliza	1	3	36–55
Townsend, Effey	1	9	24–36	Simpson, Smart (?)	8	19	55–100
Middleton, Sally	16	22	55–100	Brisbane, Flora	1	3	24–36
Flagg, Diana	8	13	55–100	Burnie, Lydia	41	75	55–100
Whaley, Rose	1	4	55–100	Salarey, Mary St.	2	4	36–55
Mushington (?), William	1	7	36–55	Holton, Elizabeth	8	14	24–36
Hannahan, Hetty	4	12	24–36	Jackson, Rachel	1	2	24–36
Williamson, Maria	1	4	55–100	Gardner, Mary	1	2	10–24
Huger, Benjamin T	8	22	36–55	Barquet, Barbara	9	22	24–36
Duprat, Hannah	2	7	36–55	Brown, Darcus	1	5	55–100
Mathews, George	13	18	55–100	Cookson, Josephine	2	8	55–100
Watson, Lydia	3	5	55–100	Gibson, Rachel	2	9	55–100
Gordon, James	2	11	36–55	Belanto, Philette	2	4	55–100
Irving, Moses	4	6	36–55	Creighton, Maria	1	5	55–100
Wright, Casar	14	15	10–24	Weston, Lydia	1	3	24–36
See, John	22	28	24–36	Jenkins, Patty	1	7	36–55
Wale, Gilbert	2	5	10–24	Drayton, Jane	17	18	55–100
Dwight, Eliza	3	5	10–24	Whitehart, Peggy	10	11	55–100
Johnston, Camilla	16	21	24–36	Hinson, Elizabeth	15	25	10–24
Smith, Eleanor	1	2	10–24	Hinson, Mary	1	2	10–24
Dubois, Rose	2	4	55–100	LaFayette, Naselye	5	6	36–55
Carado, Mary	1	4	55–100	Florin, Ann	1	6	24–36
Nelson, Peggy	1	2	24–36	LaPorte, Ellen	1	6	24–36
Cooper, Thomas J	2	5	10–24	Turner, Sarah	1	3	10–24
McBeath, John	3	7	10–24	Johnston, Catherine	2	9	55–100
Pennington, Martha	3	5	10–24	Lockwood, Henrietta	1	5	24–36
Seymour, William W	1	7	24–36	DeSage, Mary	2	5	55–100
				Duncan, Phillis	4	10	36–55
Ward No. 3				Richards, Mary	2	7	24–36
Batemen, Edward	12	14	36–55	Lloyd, Emma	4	5	24–36
DeSiesseline, Kitty	9	14	36–55	Smith, Mary	2	6	36–55
Cliss (?), Sarah	1	2	24–36	Wells, Rachel	3	4	55–100
Smith, Linda	5	8	36–55	Newton, Betsey	5	11	24–36
Brown, Jane	8	14	10–24	Brown, Malcolm	5	10	24–36
Campbell, Samuel	1	2	10–24	Lewis, Polly	1	3	24–36
LeCombe, Joseph	5	6	10–24	Jenkins, Harriot	1	7	36–55
French, Hester	2	3	10–24	Fuller, Rosetta	5	11	36–55
Ball, Sylvia	1	4	24–36	Careu, Jenny	1	2	55–100
Jackson, Ellen	3	8	24–36	Eason, James	3	14	36–55
Buckle, Maria	2	13	55–100	Levy, Affey	6	13	55–100

SOUTH CAROLINA—*Continued*

Name	Slaves	Total	Age	Name	Slaves	Total	Age
Ward No. 3—Cont.				King, Crecia	3	4	36–55
Johnson, Sophia	9	10	55–100	Freeman, Mary	3	11	24–36
McKenzie, Patience	1	10	55–100	Groning, Simons	9	14	10–24
Brown, Molly	7	9	55–100	Townsend, Tenah	2	3	55–100
Cornwell, Emele L.	3	9	55–100	Smith, Cyrus	2	7	10–24
Legare, Dolly	14	15	24–36	Garden, Martha	2	8	24–36
Bourneau, Adel	2	5	55–100	North, Priscilla	3	4	10–24
Trenne, E.	2	6	55–100	Lord, Maria	1	9	36–55
Gregorie, Adam	6	9	24–36	Taylor, Martha	3	8	10–24
Le Marr, Charles	5	8	36–55	Harrison, John	4	8	24–36
Simmons, William	2	3	36–55	Cole, Hagar	1	13	36–55
Armou, Louisa	3	6	55–100	Jones, Jehu, Jr.	1	11	55–100
Bemar, Mary	5	6	55–100	Mitchell, Ann	6	16	55–100
Watts, Mary	10	11	55–100	Savage, Henrietta	1	2	10–24
Singleton, Michl	1	2	55–100	Hollowell, Richard	8	19	55–100
Smith, Carlos	4	12	24–36	Blanchard, Charlotte	1	7	24–36
Wilson, Susan	1	3	24–36	Harrison, James	1	4	24–36
Cox, Julia	3	10	24–36	Hannahan, Hetty	2	7	24–36
Ward, Rose	5	11	55–100	Liston, Henry	2	5	24–36
Mathews, John B.	6	17	24–36	McCall, Samuel	10	13	24–36
Stevenson, Lydia	1	10	55–100	Lesessue, Betsey	4	5	10–24
Aiken, Bella	4	9	36–55	Maxwell, James	2	6	24–36
Magwood, Sandy	12	19	24–36	Veree, Elizabeth	2	4	24–36
Simons, Mary	1	5	24–36	White, Zanza	7	8	24–36
Mathews, Peter	1	7	24–36	Roberts, Venus	2	3	36–55
Jacobs, Catherine	8	33	55–100	Smith, John	3	4	24–36
Thorn, Rebecca	3	9	36–55	Jones, Benjamin	1	4	24–36
				Johnston, Sarah	1	6	24–36
Ward No. 4				Simonds, Clarissa	6	8	55–100
Barquet, Barbara	9	22	24–36	Lawrence, Benjamin	8	18	10–24
Miller, Sylvia	1	6	24–36	Lee, Grace	3	7	55–100
Langlois, Antonet	1	6	55–100	Peronneau, Datey	6	15	55–100
Francis, John	5	12	24–36	Rivers, Stephen	5	7	24–36
Johnston, James D.	6	14	24–36	Barron, Mary	1	5	36–55
Walker, Betsey	1	4	36–55	Houlton, Mary	4	11	10–24
Boyce, Rachel	6	7	10–24	Mathews, Henry B.	4	7	24–36
Lee, Elsey	2	3	24–36	De Soures, Harriot	1	4	36–55
Canter, Julietta	14	16	36–55	Ezzart, Julia	2	5	24–36
Weston, Samuel	1	5	24–36	Shaw, Sarah	6	10	24–36
Humphreys, Joseph	3	18	36–55	Cameron, Rose	4	6	36–55
Mathews, Mary	8	15	10–24	Esuard, Jane	2	4	36–55
Roberts, Cater (?)	2	3	55–100	Lewis, John	2	12	36–55
Manuel, Nancy	2	4	36–55	Beale, Sally	7	15	24–36
Brown, Ann	4	5	36–55	Cummings, James	1	5	24–36
Cole, Hagar	2	13	10–24	Berry, Mary Ann	5	6	55–100
McCall, Eliza	2	3	24–36	Philips, Ann	1	2	24–36
Ives, Sophia	1	7	36–55	White, Mary	1	3	24–36
LeSessene, F.	1	4	55–100	Badger, Portia	1	2	24–36
Smith, Angeline	12	14	36–55	Legg, William	3	7	24–36
Holmes, Maria	5	6	55–100	Turner, Philide	5	8	55–100
Barelle, Joseph	1	3	10–24	James, Emma	6	11	55–100
Pinckney, E.	7	10	36–55	Duverse, Priscilla	7	13	36–55
Drayton, Susan	2	6	55–100	Downes, Jane	4	8	10–24
Wilson, Nancy	1	4	36–55	Bridgewood, Catherine	1	6	55–100
Mitchell, Ann	10	15	55–100	Cochran, Thomas	11	14	10–24
Small, Thomas	3	8	24–36	Dart, Bella	2	6	24–36
Ross, F.	7	8	55–100	Anderson, Catherine	12	16	24–36

SOUTH CAROLINA—*Continued*

Name	Slaves	Total	Age	Name	Slaves	Total	Age
Ward No. 4—Cont.				Smith, Simon............	5	9	10–24
Kinloch, Richmond.....	2	6	36–55	North, Mary Ann.......	6	9	10–24
Francis, John...........	3	15	55–100	Michel, Assent..........	4	13	55–100
Lawrence, George.......	9	10	55–100	Wilson, Sylvia..........	10	16	36–55
Burseir, C. E...........	7	8	24–36	Belmore, Ann..........	10	14	36–55
Yeadon, Mary..........	11	14	24–36	Pope, Mary Ann........	10	15	36–55
Tucker, Samuel.........	6	10	36–55	Payne, Mary...........	10	15	55–100
Shaw, Sarah............	10	14	24–36	Cripps, Peggy..........	10	11	36–55
Izard, Isabella..........	1	5	24–36	Simons, Amelia.........	3	6	55–100
Ashe, Abraham.........	4	13	55–100	Filbin, Flora............	11	17	55–100
Shaw, Margaret........	3	4	55–100	Wilkinson, Lucy........	3	11	55–100
Moultrie, Roxana.......	1	7	24–36	Creighton, Diana.......	11	14	55–100
Young, C..............	1	3	36–55	Keith, Henry...........	7	17	24–36
Cypress, Susan.........	5	9	36–55	Busby, Mary............	10	15	24–36
				Pogson, Mary..........	9	14	24–36
CHARLESTON NECK				Buckmyer, Isaac........	3	8	24–36
Vesey, Susan...........	10	13	36–55	Holmes, Cato..........	6	15	55–100
Robinson, Betty........	10	13	36–55	Talley, Jane............	11	16	55–100
Righton, Mary.........	12	15	36–55	Furman, Mary.........	1	8	36–55
Johnston, Sophia.......	6	12	55–100	Service, James.........	2	6	55–100
Deas, Mary............	12	13	24–36	Edward, Jacob.........	10	16	36–55
Brown, Polly...........	10	14	24–36	Dewees, Sarah.........	1	5	55–100
Connor, Daffney........	1	13	55–100	Weston, John...........	1	11	36–55
Inglesby, Betty.........	11	12	36–55	De Reif, Richard.......	5	16	36–55
Ball, Nat...............	7	14	55–100	Brown, James..........	5	13	36–55
Dill, Antony...........	13	14	55–100	Drayton, Hector.......	5	16	24–36
Jervey, John...........	14	16	36–55	Dereif, Susan A........	5	10	24–36
Bell, James............	11	15	55–100	Jamiesson, John.......	2	6	36–55
Jackson, Martha........	11	15	55–100	Cross, Phoebe..........	11	13	55–100
Johnston, Hager........	11	15	55–100	Pohl, Joe..............	12	15	24–36
Franklin, Eliza.........	10	15	55–100	Edwards, Henry........	3	6	55–100
Stiemetz, Baron........	1	6	55–100	Lee, Elizabeth..........	12	14	10–24
Cordes, Rebecca........	10	13	36–55	Harleston, Nancy.......	4	9	36–55
Mott, Jacob............	1	15	36–55	Holmes, Hagar........	5	11	55–100
Clarke, James R........	12	15	24–36	Mickey, Nelly..........	1	7	36–55
Wilson, Mary..........	5	14	36–55	Edwards, James........	10	13	36–55
McIntosh, Betsey.......	10	16	55–100	Camer, Susan..........	4	14	24–36
Williams, Ann..........	11	15	36–55	Bateman, Isaac........	5	7	55–100
Delancy, Nancy........	2	5	24–36	Gregory, Mary.........	6	11	36–55
Baxter, Amos...........	1	7	36–55	Pillotte, Mary C........	14	17	55–100
Syllable, Castille........	6	7	36–55	Kelly, Margaret........	8	10	24–36
Solomon, Hannah.......	20	26	24–36	Langlois, Antonet.......	2	7	36–55
Turpin, Jane...........	1	12	24–36	Plumet, Juliet..........	3	4	24–36
Sasportes, Catherine.....	5	13	24–36	Gregory, Eleanor.......	2	6	36–55
Glen, Rachel...........	12	14	10–24	Mitchell, Crissy........	4	7	36–55
Parsons, Hannah.......	6	7	24–36	Gowan, Thomas........	10	12	55–100
Gilchrist, Martha.......	11	14	(?)	Crummell, Margaret....	1	11	55–100
Cochran, Samuel........	6	14	36–55	Antonie, Belser.........	4	8	36–55
Jones, Jeremiah.........	10	14	36–55	Legare, Susan..........	10	15	36–55
Mathews, Henry........	6	12	36–55	Henry, Charles.........	2	7	24–36
McCleod, Cato.........	2	12	55–100	Mayrant, Diana........	8	9	10–24
Mathews, Jane.........	14	17	36–55	Strobel, Thomas.......	13	15	55–100
Bercier, Charles........	10	14	36–55	Wilson, Ann............	13	16	24–36
Bolard, Eliza..........	5	15	24–36	Wall, Peter............	13	18	24–36
Liles, Maria...........	5	7	24–36	McCready, Mary.......	12	17	36–55
Gilberry, Catherine......	4	14	36–55	Fair, Pleasant..........	7	13	55–100
McKinney, William.....	4	15	55–100	Moore, Richard.........	3	16	24–36

SOUTH CAROLINA—*Continued*

Name	Slaves	Total	Age	Name	Slaves	Total	Age
CHARLESTON NECK—*Cont.*				*St. Bartholomews Parish*			
Brown, Mary...........	6	11	24–36	Horry, L., Mistress......	84	93	10–24
Jones, Cuffey...........	8	18	36–55	Seabrook, Ephraim......	44	53	36–55
Bishop, George.........	4	8	36–55	Stock, Margaret........	46	47	24–36
Tucker, Nancy.........	11	16	55–100				
Alston, Cuffey..........	13	23	55–100	*St. Paul's Parish*			
Pryor, Will.............	11	20	24–36	Logan, Jane...........	16	17	55–100
Rosenberg, Betty.......	12	17	36–55	Johnson, Henry (Esta.) .	3	7	36–55
Small, Reuben..........	11	13	24–36	Martin, George (Esta.) ..	3	8	36–55
Dallas, Benjamin.......	13	14	10–24	Dalton, Frances........	1	4	55–100
Cleaveland, Paul.......	8	14	36–55	Postell, Daniel..........	11	18	24–36
Guest, William.........	7	10	24–36				
Watson, D.............	7	14	55–100	*St. Georges Parish*			
Sayward, James........	6	11	36–55	Stevens, Lamb.........	7	9	55–100
Parlar, Peter...........	10	15	36–55				
Parker, Hager..........	9	15	55–100	EDGEFIELD COUNTY			
Lee, Elizabeth.........	3	6	36–55	Moore, Marey..........	3	10	24–36
Mitchell, Ann..........	2	5	36–55				
Wigfall, Mary..........	3	5	36–55	KERSHAW COUNTY			
Deport, Louisa.........	2	10	24–36	Harris, George.........	1	12	55–100
Mishaw, John..........	8	21	36–55	Richard, (Chestnut).....	2	3	36–55
Lamford, Jos...........	3	5	36–55	Spikes, Ceiley..........	1	8	55–100
Tardiff, William........	4	12	36–55	Scott, David...........	4	6	55–100
Johnston, Mary L.......	4	8	10–24	Taylor, Theresa........	1	2	55–100
Shilon (?), Mary........	3	4	36–55				
Marchant, Peter.......	1	10	36–55	NEWBERRY COUNTY			
Friday, William........	2	17	24–36	Brown, Charles........	4	6	55–100
Johnson, Louisa........	3	10	24–36	Felker, Nancy..........	1	2	55–100
Capers, Frank..........	2	9	55–100	Heller, Moses...........	2	3	55–100
Lyon, Thomas..........	3	5	24–36	Glouster, Jesse.........	4	5	36–55
Garden, John...........	10	18	36–55	Thompson, Jane........	2	5	10–24
Smith, Albert..........	1	5	24–36	Dennis, Lucy...........	3	5	55–100
Foster, A. W...........	14	15	24–36	Bugg, Hannah..........	1	5	24–36
Maverick, Samuel.......	6	12	36–55	Leonard, Martha.......	1	5	36–55
Oliver, Nelly...........	4	9	55–100				
				RICHLAND COUNTY			
CHESTERFIELD COUNTY				*Columbia*			
Shade, Michell..........	8	7	36–55	Patterson, Jim..........	3	7	36–55
Revells, Jno............	4	5	24–36	Bostick, Susan..........	4	8	24–36
				Moore, Sally...........	2	3	55–100
COLLETON COUNTY				Green, Peter...........	4	8	10–24
St. Johns				Mote, Rebecca.........	1	2	24–36
Angel, Justus...........	84	88	55–100	Jackson, Mary.........	2	4	24–36
				Shavers, Mary..........	1	3	24–36
St. James Goose Creek							
Brown, S..............	2	3	36–55	SUMTER COUNTY			
Russel, Richard........	2	3	24–36	Elison, William.........	4	12	36–55
Tennant, Charles.......	38	42	55–100				
Holmes, Henry.........	12	18	24–36	WILLIAMSBURGH COUNTY			
Bell, John.............	12	18	36–55	Cockfield, Hesekiah.....	2	3	10–24
Simons, James..........	5	12	36–55				
Simons, John...........	2	7	55–100	YORK COUNTY			
Simons, E. J...........	4	7	24–36	Michum, Cassy.........	1	9	36–55

TENNESSEE

Name	Slaves	Total	Age	Name	Slaves	Total	Age
BEDFORD COUNTY				Ede	1	1	24–36
Bass, John	1	10	55–100	Campbell, Philip	1	2	55–100
				Williams, Moses	2	4	36–55
DAVIDSON COUNTY				Reagan, Milly	2	3	55–100
Sherod, Bryant	4	20	36–55				
Young, Harriet	1	3	10–24	**LINCOLN COUNTY**			
Taylor, Jacob	1	2	24–36	Batey, Landon	5	6	55–100
				Smith, William	5	6	24–36
Nashville							
Bell, Buck	2	3	10–24	*Town of Fayetteville*			
Butcher, Ann	1	2	24–36	Kennedy, Allen	1	7	36–55
Childress, Dilcy	1	4	36–55	Goodlow, James	2	5	55–100
Cook, Hubbard	1	10	55–100				
Call, Joseph	3	8	36–55	**MADISON COUNTY**			
Graham, R. P.	1	5	36–55	Lane, Isaac	2	4	55–100
Hart, Samuel	1	2	55–100				
Hudson, Harry	3	6	36–55	**MAURY COUNTY**			
Jefferson, Thomas	4	5	24–36	Woodson, Cuffee	4	11	55–100
Lytle, Stephen	3	7	36–55				
Lockhart, Jefferson	1	6	24–36	**MONROE COUNTY**			
Myres, Trim	1	4	36–55	*98th Regiment*			
Martin, Albert	1	2	24–36	Crusoe, John	1	6	36–55
Mandley, Williams	1	4	24–36				
Rankin, James	1	3	36–55	**MONTGOMERY COUNTY**			
Shanklin, Johnston	2	3	24–36	Barrett, Sampson	4	7	36–55
Staggs, James	1	3	24–36	Casey, Willis	2	3	24–36
Thomas, John	3	6	24–36	Hunt, Herod	1	3	55–100
Woods, Claricy	1	7	24–36	Mayo, Quaminy	1	2	36–55
Wamack, Patience	4	6	55–100	Moore, Benjn	6	8	55–100
DICKSON COUNTY				*Clarksville*			
Dyre, Polly	1	9	10–24	Brown, Ned	1	4	55–100
				Dandridge, Agatha	5	6	55–100
GIBSON COUNTY							
Feggins, Peter	3	4	36–55	**OVERTON COUNTY**			
				Coop, Alexander	1	2	36–55
GILES COUNTY							
Henderson, Mary	1	2	24–36	**SHELBY COUNTY**			
				Kinkead, W.	1	7	55–100
GREENE COUNTY				Loiselle, A.	3	8	10–24
Davis, Thos.	1	4	55–100	Brocar, C.	7	9	55–100
				Blackwell, J.	5	6	10–24
HUMPHREYS COUNTY				Dickens, J.	1	10	36–55
Bunch, Winny	1	4	55–100	Smith, J.	1	8	24–36
JEFFERSON COUNTY				**SUMNER COUNTY**			
Elias—free	4	5	36–55	Jones, Priscilla	1	2	36–55
James and Wife (Slaves)	2	2	55–100	Hodge, Caesar	1	4	36–55
Milly—free	1	3	55–100				
Levina—free	1	2	24–36	**WHITE COUNTY**			
				Wilson, Thomas	1	5	36–55
KNOX COUNTY							
Knoxville				**WILLIAMSON COUNTY**			
Emmett, Reuben	1	6	36–55	Brooks, Gamble	11	12	36–55
Smith, Solomon	1	6	24–36				
Judy	1	1	55–100	**WILSON COUNTY**			
Phoebe	1	1	55–100	George, Polly	2	9	55–100
Beauman, Ailey	1	3	24–36	Stewart, Joseph	9	14	100–

VIRGINIA

Name	Slaves	Total	Age
ACCOMAC COUNTY			
St. Georges Parish			
Ames, Bridget	1	2	36–55
Bevans, Sheppard	1	6	24–36
Bird, Levin	1	4	55–100
Custis, Littleton	1	3	55–100
Chandler, Tamer	1	6	55–100
Chandler, Southey	2	4	36–55
Drummond, Charles	3	9	36–55
Dennis, Solomon	3	5	55–100
Elliott, Esther	1	2	36–55
Ker, Milly	1	2	36–55
Ker, Caleb	1	3	36–55
Ker, Priscilla	1	4	36–55
Leatherbury, James	2	7	55–100
Moses, Hannah	1	2	36–55
Pitts, George	2	4	24–36
Parker, Appy	1	3	55–100
Poulson, Shadrack	1	3	36–55
Parker, Simon	2	3	55–100
Poulson, William	2	3	10–24
Stokely, Betsey	1	3	55–100
Teague, Marshall	1	5	36–55
Accomack Parish			
Blake, Polly	1	5	36–55
Conquest, Thomas	2	6	55–100
Carter, Benjamine	1	2	55–100
Crippen, James	2	4	55–100
Carter, Benjamin	1	2	55–100
Duncan, Sarah	7	9	55–100
Dix, Sally	6	7	24–36
Feedaman, Eli	4	9	36–55
Fields, Elizabeth	3	5	55–100
Harman, Walter	1	5	24–36
Henderson, Levin	1	5	55–100
Outten, Selby (on farm)	4	5	10–24
Purnell, William	4	8	55–100
Piper, Henry	4	5	36–55
Selby, Meshack	1	4	55–100
Tunnell, Sarah, or Sml. Westerhouse	1	4	36–55
Rew, John (on farm)	2	3	55–100
ALBEMARLE COUNTY			
Battles, Braskin (?)	1	8	36–55
Battles, Robert	1	4	55–100
Farrar, Reuben	3	7	55–100
Fosset, Joseph	5	6	36–55
Farsley, Daniel	1	2	55–100
Harris, Charles	2	11	36–55
Kenny, Betsy	4	5	10–24
Middlebrooke, William	2	8	24–36
Scott, Jesse	1	7	36–55
AMELIA COUNTY			
Hamm, Sally	2	6	24–36

Name	Slaves	Total	Age
Ligon, Else	1	9	36–55
Hughes, Samuel	2	5	36–55
Hilton, Will	2	6	55–100
Hughes, Edith	1	2	36–55
Osborne, Nancy	1	6	10–24
Bragg, Joseph	23	25	24–36
Harriss, Nancy S.	1	3	55–100
AUGUSTA COUNTY			
Norris, Humphrey	3	4	24–36
Stepney, Peter	7	9	36–55
White, Peter	5	6	55–100
Staunton			
Ware, Daniel	1	6	36–55
BATH COUNTY			
Clark, Milly	1	3	36–55
BEDFORD			
Jackson, Nicy	2	8	55–100
Arthur, George	1	3	55–100
Hughes, John	3	9	55–100
Lewis, Bosan	2	5	55–100
BERKELEY COUNTY			
Anderson, Samuel	2	9	24–36
Compton, Solomon	1	3	55–100
Coalston, Randle	3	4	?
Furlong, Henry	6	8	100–
Logan, William	4	5	36–55
Parrot, Elenor	2	3	36–55
Sands, Hannah	2	3	55–100
BUCKINGHAM COUNTY			
Nicholas, Lucy	1	2	36–55
Hughes, Molley (?)	5	5	?
CAMPBELL COUNTY			
Bartlett, Chls	1	2	36–55
Jackson, Daniel	2	3	36–55
Lucas, Samuel	1	2	55–100
Powell, Lucy	2	6	36–55
Turner, James	2	4	24–36
Tupence, Ann	1	4	24–36
Thomas, Sally	1	9	36–55
Watts, Betsey	1	6	24–36
Howe, Isaac	2	5	36–55
Fields, Sally	2	7	55–100
Jackson, John	2	6	24–36
Jones, Richard	2	4	55–100
Jennings, Sally	1	2	36–55
CAROLINE COUNTY			
Braxton, George	1	6	36–55
Courtney, John	1	8	24–36

VIRGINIA

Name	Slaves	Total	Age	Name	Slaves	Total	Age
CHARLES CITY COUNTY				Duzard, Ann	1	9	36–55
Bailey, Robert	1	3	36–55	Chavers, Milly	1	5	36–55
Cole, Elizabeth	5	6	36–55	Pegram, Thos	4	5	55–100
Brown, William T	4	8	24–36	Ellis, Wyat	1	2	24–36
Christian, Mourning	1	2	36–55	Newney, John	1	2	36–55
CHARLOTTE COUNTY				Eppes, Peterson	3	6	24–36
Rawlins, Julius	1	3	55–100	Elliot, Thos	1	7	55–100
Jackson, Preston	1	5	24–36	Scott, Patsey	1	3	24–36
Minnis, Carroll	1	5	36–55	Burnet, Robert	1	9	24–36
Ealand, John (& W. E.)	7	8	36–55	Crook, Betty	2	3	55–100
Chavis, John	1	8	55–100	Walker, Lud	1	7	55–100
Chavis, Mack	1	3	10–24	Crook, Robert	2	11	36–55
Byrd, William	3	7	55–100	Monday, Thomas	2	6	55–100
Jackson, William	1	5	24–36	Walker, Eliza	1	4	24–36
CHESTERFIELD COUNTY				Lee, Polly	2	3	36–55
Smith, Robert	3	5	55–100	Green, Patty	1	2	36–55
Clarke, Nancy	1	4	24–36	Brown, Samuel	1	3	10–24
Cunningham, Nancy G.	1	9	36–55	Scott, Aggy	1	3	55–100
Fields, Ned	5	6	36–55	Russel, Honoria	1	6	55–100
McCreddy, Betsy	4	7	24–36	Jackson, Daniel	7	9	55–100
Cunningham, Alexander	1	4	10–24	Jeffers, Sylvia	2	7	36–55
Patterson, Sigh	1	4	36–55	Wahron, John	1	5	24–36
Morris, Elijah	3	5	36–55	Smith, Patsey	1	2	24–36
Batts, Nancy	8	10	36–55	Thomas, Susan	1	9	36–55
Gillum, Eady	1	8	36–55	Harris, Jos	1	10	10–24
Brown, Rebecker	2	3	55–100	Bailey, Aquil	6	7	36–55
Perry, Lucy	1	2	55–100	Shields, Edward	4	5	24–36
Logain, Watthall	1	7	55–100	Butler, Peggy	1	3	55–100
Gates, James R	1	2	36–55	Booker, Jack	2	3	24–36
CUMBERLAND COUNTY				Gilliam, Eady	1	10	55–100
Booker, Billy	2	4	55–100	Galleo, Frances	2	4	55–100
Drew, Jack	2	4	55–100	Eppes, James	4	7	24–36
Daniel, William	32	33	36–55	Corn, Henry	2	3	24–36
Ellison, Chloe	2	6	55–100	Harris, Jackey	2	6	24–36
Edwards, George	2	3	55–100	Coupland, Rachel	2	5	36–55
Freeman, York	2	4	36–55	Robinson, Diana	1	11	36–55
Higginbotham, Sophia	1	6	24–36	Robinson, Lavina	1	3	10–24
Kidd, Pleasant	1	6	24–36	Stuart, Peggy	1	9	36–55
Logan, Chastaine	1	3	24–36	Graves, Eliza	1	2	24–36
Mayo, Nancy	1	6	24–36	Ellerson, Sarah	3	7	24–36
Martin, Nancy	1	4	10–24	Galle, Eliza	5	6	24–36
Mayo, Robert	1	3	36–55	Galle, Amelia	2	6	36–55
Mayo, William	4	11	55–100	Quarles, Jane	2	5	36–55
Reynolds, Lewis	1	3	24–36	Molson, William	1	7	10–24
Turpin, Strato	1	3	55–100	Anter, Polly	5	7	36–55
DINWIDDIE COUNTY				Overton, Rebecca	2	4	24–36
Petersburg				Walker, William	3	11	36–55
Lawson, Booker	1	7	24–36	Bonner, Rebecca	2	3	24–36
Turner, Milly	1	11	55–100	Stuart, John	1	8	24–36
Freeman, Lenn A	1	5	55–100	Jones, Mary	2	14	55–100
King, Hannah	1	3	55–100	Smith, Esther	2	11	55–100
Scott, Daniel	2	8	36–55	Kennon, Eliza	1	2	36–55
Matthews, Bailey	1	5	24–36	Wilson, Saml	1	2	24–36
Brander, Shedr	2	10	36–55	White, Susan	1	3	36–55
				Biggins, Mary	1	5	24–36
				Martin, James	1	7	36–55
				Thomas, Isaac	1	7	36–55

VIRGINIA—*Continued*

Name	Slaves	Total	Age	Name	Slaves	Total	Age
Petersburg—Cont.				Tabb, Nancy...........	1	4	36–55
Thomson, Ann..........	1	5	24–36	Bridget, Thomas........	2	3	24–36
King, Anna............	1	7	24–36	Allen, Samuel..........	3	4	55–100
Bailey, Precilla.........	1	4	55–100	Hopson, James.........	1	10	36–55
Bailey, Eliza...........	1	9	36–55	Hampton, Bray.........	1	2	55–100
Brown, John...........	1	2	36–55	Evans, James..........	1	3	24–36
Ferrell, Polly...........	1	2	36–55				
Webster, Abby.........	1	3	24–36	ESSEX COUNTY			
Lewis, Peyton.........	3	4	36–55	Nelson, Bunday........	1	11	36–55
Eaves, Martin B........	5	11	24–36	Anky, Cole.............	1	2	55–100
Donaldson, Susan.......	1	2	55–100	McDowney, Mildred....	1	9	55–100
Dunn, Lewis.*.........	1	4	24–36	McDowney, Peter.......	1	6	24–36
Hamilton, Richard.....	3	5	24–36	Richardson, Austin......	6	8	55–100
Booker, Jack..........	4	13	55–100	Rich, William..........	1	3	24–36
Carter, Moses.........	1	8	55–100				
Jones, Fedr..........	1	2	55–100	FAIRFAX COUNTY			
Minor, Jane..........	5	6	36–55	Hathaway, James (fb)..	3	10	24–36
Edwards, George S.....	2	7	24–36	Simms, Lee (fbk).......	1	5	36–55
Eppes, William........	1	2	36–55	William, Lee (fbk).....	1	2	55–100
Valentine, John........	2	3	?	Hopkins, Keziah........	1	8	36–55
Bolling, Eliza..........	2	5	?	Lee, William L. (fbk)....	3	6	36–55
Wright, Frank.........	2	3	24–36	Stuart, James (Negro)...	9	9	55–100
Gilliam, Eady.........	1	7	36–55	Harriss, Edmond (fb)....	2	7	36–55
Lewis, Charles.........	1	4	36–55	Cromer, Dennis (fb).....	1	4	36–55
Williams, Betsy........	1	11	55–100	Honesty, John (fbk).....	1	7	36–55
Majors, Thos..........	2	6	55–100	Lyles, William (fb)	1	2	24–36
Campbell, Jack........	1	4	36–55				
Elliot, Sally...........	1	4	36–55	FLUVANNA COUNTY			
Wilson, Joseph........	1	2	36–55	Norris, Jesse...........	3	5	36–55
Perry, Lucy...........	1	2	36–55	Couzens, John..........	3	14	36–55
Brown, James.........	2	4	55–100	Couzens, Jordon........	3	4	36–55
Allen, Lucy...........	1	3	24–36	Gypson, Moses.........	1	4	55–100
Banks, Hannah........	1	4	24–36	Barnet, Charles........	1	9	36–55
Wilcox, Thos..........	1	2	55–100	Peyton, Samuel........	4	7	55–100
Bailey, Judy..........	2	4	24–36	Wood, Jeremiah........	1	4	36–55
Angus, George.........	2	7	24–36	Wood, Nelly...........	2	3	55–100
White, Milly..........	1	2	24–36	Quarles, Nelly.........	1	2	55–100
Holcomb, Benjamin.....	1	2	55–100				
Jackson, Nancy........	1	4	36–55	FRANKLIN COUNTY			
Minor, Jincey.........	8	9	36–55	Boyd, Samuel..........	1	4	55–100
Taylor, Sarah..........	3	5	10–24	Callaway, Squire........	1	5	55–100
Angus, Judy...........	1	7	55–100	Early, Elizabeth........	4	7	36–55
Fagan, Bridget........	1	5	55–100	Green, Nelly...........	1	11	36–55
Coupland, Rachel.......	2	5	55–100				
				FREDERICK COUNTY			
DINWIDDIE COUNTY				*Eastern District*			
Jones, Benson..........	4	5	24–36	Adams, Sylva..........	1	7	24–36
Freeman, Lewis........	1	3	55–100	Brady, Henry..........	6	7	24–36
Clanton, Hartwell.....	2	3	36–55	Caeser, Julius..........	1	4	55–100
Berry, Thomas	6	10	36–55	Folks, Mima...........	1	7	55–100
				Whiting, Thomas.......	5	8	55–100
ELIZABETH CITY COUNTY							
Pane, Jack.............	1	3	55–100	GLOUCESTER COUNTY			
Robbins, Daniel........	3	4	24–36	Annaka...............	1	4	55–100
Johnson, Matthew......	1	2	36–55	Bowles, Jefferson.......	2	7	24–36
Allen, Stephen.........	3	6	24–36	Chavis, Becky.........	1	4	24–36
Reid, Jeffres...........	4	6	24–36	Chevis, Kitty..........	1	6	36–55
Brown, Champion......	2	3	10–24	Dennis, Peggy..........	1	4	24–36

VIRGINIA—*Continued*

Name	Slaves	Total	Age	Name	Slaves	Total	Age
GLOUCESTER CO.—*Cont.*				Scott, Aaron	2	5	36–55
Fox, James	1	5	55–100	Spencer, Gabriel	5	6	24–36
Gregory, James	13	15	55–100	Wood, Wislon	4	6	24–36
Hearn, Ephraim	9	11	55–100	Whitlock, Phebe	1	4	55–100
Lemon, John H.	1	6	24–36	Liggon, Sally	1	2	55–100
Lemon, Eliza	1	6	24–36	Smith, Peyton	1	4	24–36
Rowe, Fanny	1	4	55–100	Housling, Edith	1	2	36–55
Rilee, Frank	1	2	36–55	Harris, Alice	1	5	55–100
Southerland, James	3	4	24–36	Ellis, Milly	4	5	36–55
Southerland, Jeremiah	1	4	36–55	Rutherford, Thomas	5	7	36–55
West, John	1	4	24–36	Harris, Thomas	1	2	10–24
Ward, Jane	1	2	55–100	King, Billy	2	3	36–55
Wilmore, Peggy	1	6	24–36	Coleman, Elizabeth	2	6	55–100
				Bluefoot, Lucey	1	6	55–100
GOOCHLAND COUNTY				Owen, Sally	1	3	55–100
Cooper, Roger	1	7	55–100	Cross, Moses	2	5	36–55
Sampson, Jacob	2	10	24–36	Cousins, Barbara	1	6	55–100
Turner, Milly	1	3	24–36	Adams, Harry	1	10	36–55
				Crenshaw, Edmund (of			
(Eastern District)				Hanover)	9	10	24–36
James, Eady	1	4	24–36	Carter, Betsy	4	7	36–55
Pearce, Milly	1	9	55–100	Harvie, J. B.	2	4	36–55
Shelton, James	1	7	24–36	Laurence, Cesar	1	3	36–55
Cousins, Henry	1	11	36–55	Price, Becky	2	4	24–36
Pearce, John	18	27	36–55	Russel, Archer	2	4	36–55
Frazier, Wat	1	3	55–100	Jones, Agness	1	2	36–55
Lynch, John	8	9	55–100	Carter, Henry	1	4	36–55
Mayo, Dinor	1	3	36–55	Hill, Robert	1	8	36–55
				Banks, Peters	2	3	24–36
GREENSVILLE COUNTY				Whistler, Betty	1	5	24–36
Hunt, Goodwin	2	16	55–100	Cowles, Thomas	2	4	24–36
Day, John	2	8	10–24	Reynolds, Dinah	2	3	55–100
Wadkins, David	11	33	36–55	Waddill, Kitty	1	8	36–55
Wadkins, Daniel	6	14	36–55	Hewlett, Michael	1	3	55–100
Jones, Eliza	1	12	36–55	Picot, Cyles	5	6	10–24
Mason, Mildred	2	3	55–100	Harris, Polly	2	3	36–55
Watkins, Robert	1	10	36–55	Selden, Cary	2	3	36–55
				Little-page, Lettitia	1	2	24–36
HANOVER COUNTY				Bailey, Betsy	2	4	36–55
Stone, Matthew, F.N.	1	3	36–55	Moore, Maria	1	4	36–55
Smart, Thomas	1	5	36–55	Ruffin's, Betsy, Estate	3	8	36–55
Burnett, Richard	3	4	55–100	Blaky's, George, Estate	1	3	24–36
Brockenbrough, William	46	47	36–55	Sprigs, Robert	3	7	36–55
Gist, Lucy, F.N.	1	4	36–55				
				City of Richmond			
HENRICO COUNTY				Anderson, Samuel	2	3	36–55
Foster, Henry (of Rich-				Bell, Kitter	1	3	36–55
mond)	2	4	24–36	Brooks, Mike	1	6	24–36
Lablong, Eleoner	1	3	24–36	Bowler, Miller	2	6	24–36
Murray, Polly	1	2	36–55	Bingley, Martha	1	2	100–
Crouch, Jaspar	2	6	36–55	Baker, Betsy	1	2	55–100
Peters, Isabella	1	6	36–55	Bohannan, Rachael	1	2	24–36
Weeks, Bristo	1	3	55–100	Brown, Nancy	1	5	55–100
Macon, Marshal	1	7	36–55	Baker, Hannah	1	2	10–24
Anderson, John	1	7	10–24	Cowlin, Isaac	1	2	24–36
Langley, Eveline	2	7	24–36	Carter, Clara	2	5	24–36
Dugard, Sally	2	5	36–55	Cole, Polly	1	2	36–55

VIRGINIA—*Continued*

Name	Slaves	Total	Age	Name	Slaves	Total	Age
City of Richmond—Cont.				*Madison Ward*			
Carter, Patsy	3	5	24–36	Armistead, Lewis	3	9	36–55
Carter, Curtis	22	25	10–24	Amos, Mahala	1	8	24–36
Deane, Charlotte	1	2	24–36	Brown, Celia	1	6	24–36
Dickson, Patsy	1	2	10–24	Billbrough, Aggy	2	4	55–100
Elson, John	1	2	36–55	Braxton, Sukey	1	2	36–55
Gilliam, Sarah	1	2	10–24	Butler, Hope	5	6	36–55
Galt, Elizabeth	2	5	24–36	Cooly, Sarah	1	9	55–100
Granger, Joseph	1	2	24–36	Courtney, Martha	1	2	55–100
Goodwyn, Moses	4	5	55–100	Cross, Fanny	1	3	24–36
Greenhow, James	1	5	36–55	Cox, Jane	1	2	36–55
Hunt, Gilbert	1	2	36–55	Cosby, James	1	6	55–100
Harris, George	3	4	36–55	Chain, Cold	2	3	55–100
Hill, Minnis	2	9	24–36	Ellet, Mary	1	2	24–36
Hawkins, Mary	1	7	24–36	Friend, Caroline	4	7	10–24
Harris, Eliza	1	3	55–100	Graves, Elizabeth P.	3	5	55–100
Harris, Milly	1	8	36–55	Harris, Rebecca	1	3	10–24
Henry, Joanna	1	5	36–55	Haxall, Philip	18	19	55–100
Harler, Jinny	1	4	24–36	Harrison, Rachel A.	1	5	24–36
Harris, Maria	1	2	10–24	Jones, Matilda	1	2	24–36
Jones, Eve	1	3	55–100	Jackson, Mary	1	2	24–36
Johnson, Nelly	1	6	36–55	Morton, Rueben	3	15	36–55
Judah, Benjn.	2	6	24–36	Madden, Walter	1	4	10–24
Jackson, John	3	4	55–100	Page, Penelope	1	4	24–36
Jackson, Ann	1	3	24–36	Page, George	2	4	55–100
Jackson, Lewis	2	5	55–100	Reynolds, Isaac	4	5	36–55
Jordan, Isham	1	4	36–55	Robertson, Henry	4	6	36–55
King, Rhody	1	3	55–100	Roney, Frederick	1	6	36–55
Loney, James	4	5	36–55	Smith, Ann	3	4	24–36
Lee, Richard	1	5	24–36	Smith, Elizabeth	1	2	10–24
McEnery, Nancy	1	2	10–24	Slow, Milly	1	3	55–100
Muse, William	4	6	36–55	Scott, China	1	3	36–55
Mitchell, Lucy	1	9	10–24	Webb, Nancy	2	3	55–100
Mayo, Nelly	1	2	100–	Williams, Milly	1	2	24–36
Marshall, Davy	1	2	36–55	Yancey, Celinda	1	6	24–36
Mitchell, Elizabeth	2	3	10–24				
Patterson, Joe	1	3	24–36	*Jefferson Ward*			
Pendleton, Nellie	1	2	55–100	Anderson, Nancy	2	3	36–55
Pleasants, Milton	6	9	36–55	Anderson, Eliza	2	5	24–36
Ross, George W.	2	9	24–36	Burke, Emmy	3	4	24–36
Randolph, Harriet	1	4	24–36	Barnett, Polly	1	5	36–55
Robertson, Philip	1	2	24–36	Brown, Hannah	1	3	55–100
Smith, Betsy	2	3	24–36	Ball, Henry	1	2	24–36
Scott, Patience	1	8	24–36	Byrd, Nancy	1	4	55–100
Swann, William	5	9	55–100	Binford, Keziah	4	7	55–100
Sampson, David	5	7	36–55	Bowson, Judy	1	2	55–100
Smith, Nancy	1	3	55–100	Carter, Charles	2	3	24–36
Selden, Winny	1	2	36–55	Cooper, Maria	3	5	24–36
Smith, Charlotte	1	3	55–100	Crump, Edward	1	4	24–36
Tinsley, Betsy	1	2	24–36	Carter, Elvira	1	3	24–36
Tillman, Luby	2	3	55–100	Cokely, Milly	1	6	24–36
Tuppence, Becky	1	3	36–55	Calbert, Martha	1	2	24–36
Vaughan, Richard	5	6	36–55	Carey, Lucy	1	4	36–55
Wilkerson, Polly	1	2	36–55	Dalney, Julia	1	2	24–36
Wales, Elizabeth	2	5	24–36	Deane, Julia	2	4	36–55
Williams, Nancy	1	2	55–100	Dickson, Patty	6	7	36–55
Yates, Sylvia	2	4	55–100	Ellis, Isham	1	8	24–36

VIRGINIA—*Continued*

Name	Slaves	Total	Age	Name	Slaves	Total	Age
Jefferson Ward—Cont.				Flud, John, fre.........	2	3	24–36
Eppes, Milly..........	1	3	24–36	Wilson, Henry, fre......	2	3	24–36
Ellis, Fleming.........	3	4	36–55	Hollaway, Dilson, fre....	1	7	36–55
Fagan, Ann...........	1	6	36–55	Purdie, Eliza, fre......	3	4	36–55
Ferguson, John........	2	4	10–24	Partrick, Judia, fre......	2	6	55–190
Graves, Richmond......	1	5	36–55	Hawkins, Nathl., fre....	10	11	36–55
George, Polly...........	1	2	10–24	Wyzell, Isham, fre			
Hall, Billy............	1	2	55–100	(Uzzell?).............	3	4	36–55
Henderson, James.......	2	13	24–36	Johnes, John, fre........	1	4	36–55
Hendley, Wilson.......	3	5	36–55	Jordan, Henry, fre......	1	2	24–36
Johnson, John J........	3	5	36–55	Tynes, Fanny, fre.......	1	3	10–24
Johnson, Moses........	1	3	36–55	Tynes, Jenny, of Clo (?)			
Lewis, John...........	3	9	36–55	fre.................	1	3	55–100
Lewis, John...........	1	2	55–100	Tynes, Nancy, fre.......	1	8	36–55
Lightfoot, Armistead....	3	4	24–36	Tynes, Rebecca, fre.....	2	14	55–100
Maxwell, Julia.........	2	3	10–24	Pool, James, fre........	1	2	36–55
Morris, Wilson.........	1	5	24–36	Hollaway, Sampson, fr..	1	8	24–36
Morris, Reuben........	3	4	24–36	Wilson, Edy, fre........	1	9	36–55
Miller, Polly..........	1	2	36–55				
Munford, Patty........	1	7	55–100	JAMES CITY COUNTY			
Oliver, Ann...........	1	2	24–36	Tyler, George..........	1	9	36–55
Price, Isham..........	1	2	36–55				
Ricks, Cyrus..........	1	4	24–36	JEFFERSON COUNTY			
Robertson, Taylor......	3	4	24–36	(*Western District*)			
Rix, Jesse.............	1	3	24–36	Richardson, Cyrus......	3	13	55–100
Scott, Mary...........	1	2	10–24	Gust, John.............	5	7	36–55
Stewart, Billy.........	6	7	24–36				
Smith, Eliza...........	1	4	24–36	KING & QUEEN COUNTY			
Thomas, Betsy........	1	3	24–36	Deleaver, William.......	2	4	36–55
Tillman, Luby.........	3	4	55–100	Gilmour, Ben..........	1	10	36–55
Taylor, Nathl..........	3	4	10–24	Ham, Shadrick.........	3	4	24–36
Vines, Isaac..........	3	4	55–100	Hill, Lucy.............	7	8	55–100
Wallace, Nathan.......	2	5	24–36	Harris, Ransom.........	5	9	36–55
Woodson, Jim.........	1	2	36–55	Dungy, Polly..........	1	5	36–55
				Carter, Caty...........	1	10	36–55
ISLE OF WIGHT COUNTY				Gilmour, Fanny........	1	8	36–55
(*Eastern District*)				Hill, Hetty............	2	5	24–36
Short, Sam, fre........	1	3	24–36	Chapman, Lewis........	1	7	24–36
Green, John, fre.......	1	7	36–55	Gilmour, Elliott........	4	5	24–36
Crocker, Agga, fre.....	1	3	10–24	Goulman, Willis........	5	7	55–100
Christain, Ben, fre.....	3	5	55–100	Harris, Grace..........	1	12	55–100
Jordan, Biner, fre......	1	3	55–100	Kidd, Hannah..........	1	4	55–100
Newby, Milly, fr.......	1	9	36–55	Cole, Betsy............	1	4	55–100
Ash, Charles, fre.......	1	5	36–55				
Hill, Betty, fre........	1	3	36–55	KING GEORGE COUNTY			
Barlow, Abraham, fre...	1	15	36–55	Kendall, Elzey..........	1	4	36–55
Baker, Belinda, fre.....	1	5	55–100	Pestridge, William Henry	6	8	24–36
Tynes, Nancy, fre.......	2	13	36–55	Scott, Polly............	1	9	36–55
Johnson, Scotland, fre...	2	6	55–100	Tolson, Dennis.........	1	3	55–100
Crump, John C. (Surry).	11	12	36–55	Taylor, Benjamin O.....	71	78	10–24
Callvert, Abba, fre.....	4	5	55–100				
Floyd, Violet, fre.......	2	3	55–100	KING WILLIAM COUNTY			
Hollaway, Sally, fre.....	1	8	24–36	Anderson, James........	1	4	55–100
Wills, Jesse, fre........	3	6	55–100	Bradby, Jesse..........	1	6	36–55
Hollaway, Dinah, fre....	1	9	36–55	Sweat, Joanna..........	2	6	36–55
Hollaway, Betty, fre....	2	3	24–36				

VIRGINIA—*Continued*

Name	Slaves	Total	Age	Name	Slaves	Total	Age
LANCASTER COUNTY				NANSEMOND COUNTY			
Adams, Daniel.........	2	3	55–100	Amelia of Sawyer.......	1	5	24–36
Fauntelroy, Duke.......	1	3	55–100	Jacob of Holt...........	3	6	36–55
Weaver, Moses.........	3	10	36–55	Jacob of Read & white			
Hurst, John............	2	6	24–36	wife.................	2	9	36–55
				Jack of Hawksey........	1	4	36–55
LOUDON COUNTY				Anthony of Pugh.......	3	10	55–100
Cameron Parish				Sally of Pearce.........	1	6	24–36
Clemmon, H., F.N.....	2	5	24–36	Oxford of Brewer.......	3	7	100–
Robison, Cupit, F.N....	1	3	55–100	Nancy of Hare.........	2	4	24–36
				Thomas of Bowsar......	1	7	55–100
Shelburn Parish				Hetty of Walker........	2	6	10–24
Hull, John, F.N........	1	10	55–100	Arrenia of Cowling & C..	1	5	55–100
Selva, Esther, F.N......	4	8	36–55	Gibson of Burket.......	2	3	24–36
Gale, Dugless, F.N......	2	4	36–55	Geo. of Walker.........	2	3	24–36
Corben, Milly, F.N......	5	7	55–100	Absalum of Whillock....	3	5	55–100
Doe, William, F.N......	1	4	55–100	Jack of Brown..........	1	4	10–24
Jackson, Jesse, F.N.....	1	6	10–24	Joseph of Walker.......	1	4	24–36
Mitchell, James, F.N....	5	8	24–36	John of Walker (Senr.)..	1	8	55–100
Ellzey, James, F.N......	1	4	55–100	Jack of Atkins..........	2	12	55–100
Cross, Stephen, F.N.....	2	3	55–100	Betty of Campbell......	4	6	24–36
				Polly of Manly.........	1	3	55–100
LOUISA COUNTY				Jim of Elliot...........	1	8	24–36
Mosby, Pleasant, F.N. ..	3	8	36–55	Wilson of Teamer.......	1	5	24–36
Mosby, Samuel, F.N.....	6	7	24–36	London of White.......	4	8	36–55
Wilkerson, Peggy.......	4	11	24–36	Peggy of Jordan........	1	4	36–55
Poindexter, Daniel, F.N..	2	16	36–55	Sally of Cowling........	1	4	36–55
Moore, Hezekiah, F.N...	1	4	36–55	Bob of Scott...........	3	4	36–55
Kinney, William, F.N....	1	11	55–100	Watson of Bowsar......	1	5	36–55
Edwards, Dicy, Jr., F.N.	1	4	24–36	Elvy of Ash............	5	6	36–55
Joen, Anny, F.N........	3	4	55–100	Jim of Bowsar Sen......	1	7	55–100
				John of Norfleet........	1	4	55–100
LUNENBURG COUNTY				Holliway of Copeland ...	3	6	36–55
Epes, Edward (F.N.) ...	4	10	36–55	Bill of Griffin..........	1	2	36–55
Evans, Thomas (F.N.) ..	3	6	55–100	Syphe of Matthews &			
Hitchins, Nancy (F.N.) .	1	6	55–100	white wife...........	1	2	24–36
Archer, James (F.N.) ...	4	5	36–55	Jerry of Johnson........	1	4	24–36
				Amia of Holland........	3	4	55–100
MATHEWS COUNTY				Edith of Crocker........	1	5	55–100
Callis, Sally............	2	6	55–100	Rachel of Shepherd......	1	7	24–36
				Saml of Hacket.........	2	9	36–55
MECKLENBURG COUNTY				Dempsy of Stallings			
Ivy, Prissilla...........	5	13	55–100	(Slave)...............	6	8	36–55
				David of Holland (Jr.)...	2	5	36–55
MIDDLESEX COUNTY				Charles of Crews........	2	3	55–100
Cassity, James.........	1	3	36–55	Peggy of West..........	3	4	36–55
Cole, Penny............	2	6	36–55	Bridget of Godwin......	3	4	55–100
Gowin, Nancy..........	1	2	55–100	Nancy of Shepherd......	1	4	24–36
Hord, Benjamin........	8	9	10–24	Mourning of Wilkins....	1	4	55–100
Rylee, Charles..........	1	2	55–100	Rebecka of Catchen (?)..	1	8	55–100
Thomas, Lancaster......	1	7	36–55	Lieucy of Winslow......	1	4	36–55
West, Daphny..........	4	5	55–100	Jerry of Whitfield.......	1	4	24–36
West, Priscilla..........	6	7	100–				
Peters, Betsy...........	1	3	55–100	NELSON COUNTY			
MONTGOMERY COUNTY							
Langhorn, William......	7	10	10–24	Arnold, Robert.........	1	10	55–100

VIRGINIA—Continued

Name	Slaves	Total	Age	Name	Slaves	Total	Age
NEW KENT COUNTY				Miller, Willm	2	4	55–100
Dungee, Jesse (F.c.p.)	1	5	36–55	Joseph, Lilly	3	6	36–55
Fox, Sally (F.c.p.)	2	5	55–100	Allen, Stephen	2	5	24–36
Fox, Sukey (F.c.p.)	1	5	36–55	Baucher, Desebri	4	6	24–36
Fox, Thomas (F.c.p.)	1	5	24–36	Wiles, James	2	6	24–36
Johnson, Ned (F.c.p.)	3	5	55–100	Eastwood, Jupiter	3	8	24–36
Lewis, Roger (F.c.p.)	4	6	36–55	Gibbs, Toney	1	4	24–36
Meekins, Peggy (F.c.p.)	1	2	55–100	Herbert, Sally	2	2	36–55
Ozborne, Squire (F.c.p.)	1	8	55–100	Williams, James	3	4	24–36
Pearman, Michael				Delaware, Amy	4	5	24–36
(F.c.p.)	5	15	36–55	Shuster, Hannah	1	2	36–55
Pearman, Thomas				Hunter, Sarah	1	3	55–100
(F.c.p.)	2	11	36–55	Ivey, Nelly	1	3	36–55
Parke, Hannah (F.c.p.)	3	5	55–100	Smith, Peggy	2	3	55–100
NORFOLK COUNTY				Naylor, Ann	1	2	36–55
Bressie, Lucy	4	7	24–36	Rogers, Adrian	1	5	55–100
Halstead, Isriael	3	6	24–36	Caucey, Nancy	1	8	100–
Watts, Jesse	1	4	10–24	Banks, Phillis	1	2	36–55
Elliot, Bill	1	4	36–55	Magnieu, Lovey	1	2	36–55
Shepherd, Nancy	1	9	36–55	Hancock, Arthur	3	8	24–36
Billey, Samuel	1	2	55–100	Hunter, Nancy	3	10	55–100
Pitt, Nancy	1	4	24–36	Hancock, Priscilla	5	8	55–100
Cornick, Peggy	1	2	36–55	English, Priscilla	1	5	24–36
Laverence, Juan Pedre	1	3	24–36	Miller, Robert	2	3	24–36
Nash, Aggy	1	3	10–24	Fuller, William	1	9	36–55
Bressie, Reitta	1	3	36–55	Smith, Hannah	2	5	55–100
Jones, William	3	4	36–55	Clayton, Moses	4	6	10–24
Godwin, Benjamin	1	7	36–55	Singleton, Jim	3	4	55–100
Scott, Mary	1	3	36–55	Lewis, Sam	2	5	36–55
Cooper, Charles	4	5	24–36	Ruffin, Evelina	2	6	36–55
Dixon, Mingo	2	3	24–36	Fentress, David	1	6	36–55
Sample, Nanny	1	4	55–100	Randall, Moses	1	2	36–55
Smith, Fanny	1	4	24–36	Rae, Betty	2	6	36–55
Hoggard, Thummer	15	21	36–55	Nimmo, Paul	4	9	24–36
Wilkinson, Jesse	4	5	55–100	Saunders, Allsey Ann	1	4	55–100
Africa, Wright	1	3	36–55	Ball, Sarah	1	3	55–100
NORFOLK BORO,				Roundtree, Anthony	2	4	24–36
NORFOLK COUNTY				Dixon, Thomas	1	6	24–36
Lucy	1	2	55–100	Voyart, John	2	6	36–55
Haines, Cuffey	1	3	55–100	Berry, Jane	1	3	10–24
White, Patience	1	8	55–100	Bligh, John	3	7	36–55
Cooper, George	3	4	55–100	Nicholson, Katy	3	5	36–55
Johnson, Lamb	4	5	55–100	Reed, Luke	1	5	24–36
Walke, Arthur	1	2	55–100	Shepherd, Frank	1	2	36–55
Travers, Peggy	1	4	55–100	Carr, Patsey	1	4	55–100
Ingram, Billy	1	3	55–100	Sawyer, Mary	7	8	55–100
Walker, America	1	6	55–100	Boucher, Agnes	1	2	24–36
Landford, Soloman	1	5	36–55	Collins, Racheal	4	5	55–100
Green, Hurt	3	5	24–36	Robertson, Joe	2	4	24–36
Hodges, Matt	2	5	36–55	Taylor, John	1	4	24–36
Jasper, Lucy	2	9	?	West, Beverly	2	8	36–55
Spencer, John	2	4	36–55	Gilmore, Henry	2	13	36–55
Suckey, Aunt	5	6	24–36	Vickery, Ned	6	4	36–55
Bailey, Joe	2	6	36–55	Nancy & Lydia	1	4	55–100
Slaughter, Stephen	4	5	55–100	Bligh, James	2	5	36–55
Bobee, Felix	4	6	24–36	Jordan, Moses	4	10	36–55
				Carey, Daniel	1	5	36–55

VIRGINIA—*Continued*

Name	Slaves	Total	Age	Name	Slaves	Total	Age
NORFOLK BORO, NORFOLK COUNTY—*Cont.*				*Market Square* Lee, Judy	2	3	36–55
Newby, Jacob	2	4	36–55				
Williams, Maria	1	3	36–55	ORANGE COUNTY			
Henly, Charlotte	5	12	24–36	Long, Betsy	1	7	36–55
Richardson, Lucinda	1	4	36–55	Rolls, William	5	8	36–55
Cuthbert, Matilda	2	4	24–36				
Harman, Hannah	3	5	36–55	PITTSYLVANIA COUNTY			
Singleton, Frank	3	8	10–24	Robertson, Faith	1	7	36–55
Camp, Jacob	2	3	36–55	Booker, Jessee	1	3	36–55
Tines, Patience	1	7	36–55	Wimbish, Chas	1	3	55–100
Boush, Nancy	5	7	55–100	Wisdom, George	1	2	55–100
Bonney, Aunt	1	6	55–100				
Wright, Amy	3	7	24–36	POWHATAN COUNTY			
Robertson, James	9	10	55–100	Ellis, Nancy	2	9	55–100
Ashley, Jenny	2	6	55–100				
Copelan, Seny (?)	2	4	24–36	PRINCE EDWARD COUNTY			
Jasper, Elizabeth	1	6	24–36	Homes, Lucy	1	9	36–55
Thomas, Molly	1	3	55–100	White, Toney	1	2	55–100
Newsum, Basset	1	4	36–55	White, Sam	1	17	55–100
Scott, Louisa	1	6	24–36	Epperson, Rody	2	3	55–100
Baker, Parish	2	4	24–36	Morton, Thomas A.			
Jackson, Manuel	1	3	55–100	(Cumberland)	45	49	24–36
Banks, Mary	1	2	36–55				
Gibson, Ottway	2	11	24–36	PRINCE GEORGE COUNTY			
Seaman, Tamer	1	6	36–55	Walthal, John B	2	5	55–100
White, Anthony	1	2	10–24	Gilliam, Mary Ann	1	5	24–36
Howard, Frank	2	3	24–36	Davis, Julia	4	6	24–36
Boucher, Lewis	2	4	55–100	Eppes, Eliza	3	10	24–36
Curtis, Lavina	1	13	36–55	Smith, John	1	4	36–55
Hays, William	1	6	36–55	Smith, Drury	2	5	36–55
Locust, Katy	1	4	24–36	Batte, Fanny	2	6	55–100
				Damsel, Samuel	3	4	36–55
Queen Street				Chance, James	1	5	55–100
Boyd, Nancy	1	3	36–55	Sykes, World	1	5	55–100
				Lee, Richard	3	2	36–55
Charlotte & Bute Streets							
Connor, Susan	2	4	24–36	PRINCESS ANNE COUNTY			
Jones, Cyrus	1	6	24–36	Owens, Tait	1	6	55–100
				Sparrow, Corinna	1	3	24–36
Free Mason Street				White, Sonnon (?)	1	6	36–55
Keeling, Ned	5	14	24–36	Barnes, Tom	1	9	24–36
				Fentress, Nanny	1	3	100–
Little Water Street & Vicinity				Woodhouse, George	6	7	36–55
Palmer, John	4	5	36–55	Anderson, Jack	2	3	36–55
Smith, Daniel	2	3	36–55	Smith, Jane	1	3	24–36
Commerce Street				PRINCE WILLIAM COUNTY			
Byrd, Sally	4	5	55–100	Carr, Daniel	2	4	55–100
Mandeville, John C	3	8	55–100	Kendall, Thornton	4	10	36–55
Cocke, Joseph	3	10	24–36				
				RICHMOND COUNTY			
Main Street				Hall, Peter	1	2	55–100
Williams, Jane	1	4	36–55	Newman, Louisa	1	3	55–100
Robertson, James	2	10	36–55	Lancaster, Nancy	1	3	55–100
Knight, Thomas	1	8	55–100	Bragg, Keziah	2	3	55–100
Slaughter, Betsey	1	5	24–36	Barnes, Simon	3	4	55–100

VIRGINIA—*Continued*

Name	Slaves	Total	Age	Name	Slaves	Total	Age
RICHMOND CO.—*Cont.*				**SURRY COUNTY**			
Allen, Frank...........	5	8	36–55	Scott, Nicholas G.......	1	11	36–55
Saws, Chris............	1	2	55–100	Browne, Mariah........	1	6	24–36
Veney, Jessee..........	1	5	24–36	Hardy, Simus..........	5	6	36–55
ROCKBRIDGE COUNTY				Jonathan, Molly........	1	2	55–100
Henry, John...........	2	3	36–55	Cocke, Ceasar..........	7	8	36–55
Sims, John.............	4	7	36–55	Banks, Benjamin.......	4	12	55–100
Rachael...............	3	3	36–55	Tines, James...........	1	4	36–55
Henry, William........	4	6	36–55	Pritlow, William.......	2	12	36–55
Jackson, Reuben.......	1	3	24–36	Cornwell, Tom.........	1	7	24–36
				Deborix, Anny........	1	5	36–55
SHENANDOAH COUNTY							
Woodstock, County seat				**SUSSEX COUNTY**			
Edwards, Prince........	1	6	24–36	Canada, John..........	1	5	55–100
				Hill, Frederick........	4	7	36–55
1st Batts. of 13 7 97				Parkam, Jesse..........	3	4	24–36
Regtms.				Turner, Olive..........	1	8	55–100
Spencer, Edward........	5	6	36–55	Hill, Charles..........	3	6	36–55
Tasker, Eward.........	1	3	36–55	**WESTMORELAND COUNTY**			
				Asten (?), Jerry	1	4	24–36
2nd B. 13 Rt.				Bradley, Arthur........	1	4	55–100
Bailey, James..........	1	2	36–55	Bradley, Lucy..........	1	3	10–24
				Bundy, William........	1	5	10–24
SOUTHAMPTON COUNTY				Bailey, Fanny..........	1	8	24–36
Turner, Edith..........	1	5	55–100	Jackson, Cupid.........	1	3	55–100
Taylor, Perry...........	1	3	55–100	Wright, Isaac..........	1	9	36–55
SPOTTSYLVANIA COUNTY				**WYTHE COUNTY**			
Anderson, Catharine....	3	9	36–55	Pool, Nelly.............	1	4	36–55
Garnett, Caesar........	1	5	24–36				
Johnson, Alsey.........	1	9	36–55	**YORK COUNTY**			
Simmons, Sthresley (?)..	1	9	24–36	Johnson, William.......	3	4	55–100
Brown, Maria..........	1	6	55–100	Foredice, Patsey........	2	3	36–55
Brooke, Lucy..........	1	4	36–55	Bassett, William........	3	4	55–100
Catlet, Jane...........	1	3	36–55	Dipper, John...........	4	6	36–55
Debaptist, Nancy.......	7	12	36–55	Debrix, Mary..........	2	9	36–55
Harrison, Suckey.......	1	4	55–100	Porter, Richard........	2	6	24–36
Miller, Armstead.......	2	3	36–55	Williams, Godfrey......	1	9	55–100
Wilkins, James.........	2	7	55–100	Deavenport, Anthony...	3	9	36–55
Waning, William.......	3	8	24–36	Yates, William C.......	6	8	36–55
White, Robert..........	4	8	10–24	White, Benjamin.......	1	2	55–100
STAFFORD COUNTY				China, Ceaser..........	3	5	55–100
Bossy (?), Nancy.......	3	4	36–55	Barber, James.........	6	10	36–55
Guin, Tom.............	1	5	55–100	Minor, John............	6	8	55–100
Froggett, John.........	2	3	55–100	Williams, Henry.......	1	5	36–55
Howard, Abra:........	11	21	24–36	Waller, Littleton........	28	29	55–100
Walker, Alexr..........	7	8	10–24	Jarvis, Thomas........	6	7	24–36
Jones, Chars..........	1	4	55–100	Jarvis, John............	3	7	10–24
Butler, Seth..........	1	5	24–36	Jarvis, Susan...........	1	2	55–100
Arnold, Lewis..........	2	3	36–55	Morris, George.........	6	9	36–55

ABSENTEE OWNERSHIP OF SLAVES IN THE
UNITED STATES IN 1830

Scholars have for a number of years desired documentary evidence as to the extent of absentee ownership of slaves in the United States. When slavery was attacked during the ante-bellum period, defenders of the institution often published dissertations showing how close the relations were between master and slave. On the other hand, the anti-slavery groups contended that the facts to the contrary were overwhelmingly in support of the conclusion that there was such a little of such social contact, that the Negro slave tended toward social degradation as the institution became further removed from the patriarchal state.

In this study the Department of Research of the Association for the Study of Negro Life and History has had the opportunity to extract from the census records of 1830 the names of the absentee owners of slaves in the United States at that time. As the history of slavery easily shows the tendency toward an increase in the number of such owners, this report of 1830 will evidently present the situation when slavery had its best chance to make a case for itself. The extent to which this sort of ownership prevailed will serve in the main as an index to the social contact of the master and slave classes.

In going through these records, the student will observe that few of the slave States were free of this evil of a disproportionate number of absentee owners, considered in the light of the defense of slavery. Some of these commonwealths, of course, had developed further in this direction than others. Slavery had in many places become a business, which in the economic development of this country had to employ the same processes used in any other endeavor. The slave tended to pass from the mind as a human being, and to appear more like goods and chattels.

The situation in 1830 was not exactly like that nearer the Civil War. There were comparatively few cases of absentee ownership of large groups of slaves in the District of Columbia, Delaware, Kentucky, Tennessee, or Missouri in

1830. Most cases of this sort in Maryland were small groups. The situation in Virginia and North Carolina was little different from that in Maryland. Louisiana in this respect was an exception to the rule. Alabama, Florida and Mississippi, like some of the other States, had not developed sufficiently by that time to warrant a proper estimate of their situation. Georgia showed many evidences of the tendency toward absentee ownership. It was very pronounced in South Carolina.

Absentee ownership, however, did not always mean that the Negro was thereby inconvenienced or degraded. A master often permitted certain slaves to live by themselves in the discharge of some special duty in which they had shown unusual capacity. Such groups of slaves, as the records will show, were usually small, consisting mainly of a man and his family. There are many cases of one Negro slave living by himself. An investigation shows that some of such Negroes were practically free or were working out their freedom on liberal terms.

These records, moreover, are not clear on many points which the student would like to understand. In cases of one or two slaves it is sometimes difficult to determine whether the name is that of the absentee owner or that of the slave in charge of the establishment. These same records give the names of slaves occasionally regarded as heads of families. Where it is not specifically stated that they are slaves, there often appear such names as Aunt Violet, Black John, Jupiter, or Cato. These, of course, were names usually given Negroes.

In the case of an estate of some one recently deceased, it is also doubtful whether the white persons on the plantation were serving in the capacity of overseers and managers, or were the actual heirs of the deceased. Where the whole group consists of slaves, however, the absentee ownership is clear and the overseer himself was usually a slave. In some other cases the records show that the overseer was a free Negro.

There are many cases of large groups of slaves with only one white person among them. Such a white person might have been either the owner or the overseer. As the records do not make this clear, however, they have been omitted here.

ALABAMA

Name	Slaves	Total	Name	Slaves	Total
Autauga County			Arthur F. Hopkins.........	47	47
F. Ashurst................	24	24	William Booth.............	41	41
			Jesse H. Croom............	41	41
Baldwin County			Willie Croom..............	24	24
Mary Weatherford........	13	13	William Dearing...........	174	174
			Harris Tinker	43	43
Clarke County			Aldridge Myatt...........	16	16
Murdock Murphy..........	6	6			
John B. Burke.............	4	4	**Limestone County**		
Adam Carson..............	15	15	Elisha Rice...............	26	26
D. R. W. Mc.Rea.........	14	14	Isaac Campbell............	2	2
Abner Denard.............	5	5	David Dancy..............	35	35
Joseph Parker.............	26	26			
Sarah Carter..............	4	4	**Lowndes County**		
John Weatherford..........	24	24	Elizabeth Parnett.........	5	5
Joseph Sheumore..........	7	7	Todd Robinson............	9	9
Margaret Tate.............	27	27			
Samuel Fisher.............	4	4	**Madison County**		
Thos. Burns...............	4	4	*1st and 2nd ranges of Town-*		
Henry Davis..............	40	40	*ships in Madison County*		
William Davis.............	1	1	Samuel Brown's Estate......	80	80
Thomas G. Holmes.........	6	6	Nelson Burton (overseer for		
Lewis English.............	4	4	B. S. Pope.).............	41	41
Robert Singleton...........	8	8	Pleasant Merril (overseer for		
			Major Gones)...........	17	17
Conecuh County			Wiley Thompson, for Mrs. M.		
James C. Hodges..........	5	5	Walker................	54	54
Starke H. Boyakin's (Slaves).	24	24			
Enoch Parsons (Slaves).....	38	38	*3rd and 4th Ranges of Town-*		
Thomas and Mary Boyakins.	22	22	*ships in Madison County*		
Francis Boyakins ag't for T.			William H. Campbell.......	11	11
Salmon.................	51	51			
			Fifth Range of Townships in		
Dallas County			*Madison County*		
Sarah Pooser.............	6	6	Thomas Turner............	66	66
John Taylor (deceased).....	84	84	Andrew Beirne............	64	64
M. and R. Gardner........	44	44	Sugars Turner............	6	6
Franklin County			**City of Mobile**		
Jas. R. Lockhart...........	25	25	Polly Taylor..............	4	4
Jas. T. Sanford............	53	53	Wm Holly	1	1
William O. Perkins........	64	64	David Hawkins............	1	1
J. S. Bryum..............	22	22			
Sam'l C. Rutherford........	4	4	**Monroe County**		
			Allen Clarke..............	7	7
Jackson County					
West of the 4th Range Line			**Montgomery County**		
James P. Nawlin...........	2	2	Leonard Marbury..........	6	6
			Thomas Finley (manager)....	23	24
Lauderdale County			Jno. Sikes (manager for M.		
Joseph Allen..............	9	9	B. Harris)..............	65	72
Gillen Folles..............	9	9	Thomas Harris (Overseer)...	18	19
Devenport Larthem........	16	16	Geo. Tankersley (overseer)...	18	23
James Read..............	36	36	Moses Ellison (manager)....	10	16
			William Taylor (overseer)...	45	46
Lawrence County			Nancy Lewis..............	16	16
Elizabeth Mosely..........	24	24	N. Rogers (overseer)........	31	31

ALABAMA—*Continued*

Name	Slaves	Total	Name	Slaves	Total
MONTGOMERY CO.—*Cont.*			Samuel Strudwick.........	20	20
E. Cranford (overseer for A.			COUNTY OF TUSCALOOSA		
of C.).................	21	21	Marion Banks.............	23	23
I. A. Boles, manager for Mrs.			Francis Nemo.............	4	4
Brown.................	3	10	James Goodwin............	4	4
A. B. Greene.............	1	1	G. G. Griffin.............	2	2
Elizah Friener.............	3	3			
			WILCOX COUNTY		
PERRY COUNTY			Calvin Dow...............	12	12
Middleton G. Woods........	49	49	Henry Spencer............	9	9

ARKANSAS TERRITORY

Name	Slaves	Total	Name	Slaves	Total
CRITTENDON COUNTY					
William Parsons..........	7	7	James A. Hart............	6	6

DELAWARE

Name	Slaves	Total	Name	Slaves	Total
COUNTY SUSSEX					
Baltimore Hundred					
Leah Hall................	5	5	Levinah Holland..........	4	4

DISTRICT OF COLUMBIA

Name	Slaves	Total	Name	Slaves	Total
Washington			Jeremiah Smith...........	5	5
H. Lylse.................	7	7	Lloyd Williams...........	1	1
S. Bell..................	9	9	Johnson Jackson..........	4	4
J. Shore.................	4	4			
H. Hanson...............	1	1	*Georgetown*		
D. Ross.................	2	2	Wm. Brown..............	7	7
Staunton................	1	1	Henson Jurdon...........	4	4
Lee.....................	4	4	Clare Knight.............	2	2
Jno. Brown..............	1	1	Lucy Jenkins.............	4	4
D. Atkins...............	5	5	Hanna Reintzel...........	3	3
R. Wilson...............	4	4	Letty Sprigg.............	2	2
S. Williams..............	4	4	Nancy Brown.............	4	4
L. Forrest...............	5	5	Chas. Robertson..........	1	1
Charles Bener............	4	4	Geo. Jackson.............	1	1
Nelson Harris............	2	2	Peter Thomas............	1	1
Nancy Cokely............	3	3	Josh. Woodland..........	9	9
Harriet Waters...........	5	5	Josh Crawford...........	2	2
Mary Murray............	8	8	Dolly Williams..........	5	5
Theophilus Rounds........	1	1	Kelly Mills..............	5	5
Lucy Mason.............	4	4	Jane Edinboro............	2	2
Margaret Jackson.........	6	6			
Maddox's Negroes........	2	2	ALEXANDRIA COUNTY		
Nancy Minor.............	2	2	Allen Scott..............	5	5
Harry Jackson...........	4	4	Austin Alexander.........	2	2
Robert Bean.............	4	4	Walter Jones.............	4	4
John Herbert.............	1	1	John D. Harrison.........	3	3
James Crandell...........	2	2	George Wise..............	4	4
Nathan Ingram...........	3	3			
Peter McCoy.............	1	1	*Town of Alexandria*		
Wm. Morse..............	2	2	Richard M. Scott.........	6	6
John T. Smith...........	7	7			
Eliza Howard............	3	3	WASHINGTON COUNTY		
Wm. Saunders...........	8	8	Ths. Parsifal Overseer......	19	26
Rachael Dagg............	11	11	Paul Brown..............	4	4
Ann Graham............	5	5	Catharin Foxall...........	3	3
Araminti Carval..........	6	6	Jos. Calder..............	5	5

FLORIDA

Name	Slaves	Total	Name	Slaves	Total
DUVAL COUNTY			NASSAU COUNTY		
Demsy Bynum............			Maria Osborne............	11	11
John Crictton's Overseer....	6	11	ST. JOHNS COUNTY		
			Mathew J. Keith..........	43	44
ESCAMBIA COUNTY			Gabriel W. Perpall........	39	40
William T. Kilber..........	6	6	*Matanzas River*		
			Antonio Rulant............	4	4
LEON COUNTY			*North River*		
Gabriel Parker.............	6	6	Joseph Baya..............	3	3
Alber R. Garnett..........	7	7			

GEORGIA

Name	Slaves	Total	Name	Slaves	Total
BALDWIN COUNTY			CHATHAM COUNTY		
Nilry & Baxter............	52	52	*Cherokee Hill District*		
Hugh Craft (Negroes).......	9	9	J. P. Williamsons' Slaves....	192	192
P. R. Young (Negroes).....	29	29	Jacob Reed's Slaves........	225	227
Watkins (for Carter)........	106	107	Joseph Stiles Slaves........	57	58
S. Roberts (for Calhoun).....	29	30	Ann Goldsmith............	6	6
			W. W. Gordon's Slaves.....	64	65
BRYAN COUNTY			Richard Stiles' Slaves.......	47	48
Edward Bond.............	3	3	John M. Berien's Slaves.....	96	100
			Thomas Young Slaves......	302	308
BURKE COUNTY			James Wilkins Slaves.......	51	52
O. Wm. Schley............	19	19	A. Jelfair's Slaves..........	47	47
			Estate of F. McLerron......	83	83
67th Company District					
Nathaniel Beall............	11	11	*Ogeechee District*		
William Lovell. o..........	44	52	Estate of F. Cronvoise......	45	45
James I. W. Davis.........	10	10	Wm. B. Bullock's Slaves.....	81	84
			M. H. McAllister's Plant....	74	75
62nd District			Eliza Lloyd's Plantation	48	49
Samuel Preskitt. o.........	41	44	Daniel Blake's Plantation....	186	191
			Geo. Anderson, Plantation...	161	162
60th District			Geo. W. Anderson, Plantation	38	38
John H. Cox. o.............	75	77	Geo. W. Owen's Plantation..	86	87
Stephen Harrell o..........	17	23	James Marshal's Plantation..	68	68
John R. Prescott..........			Mary Savage Plantation	48	49
" O., A. Walker.........	44	44	F. H. McLeod Slaves.......	132	132
Howell Hargrove..........			James Browne Slaves.......	66	67
" O., A. Walker........	74	74	Dr. R. Elliott's Slaves......	67	67
Thomas Agerton...........			Heirs of S. Elliott..........	129	130
" O., Wm. Urguhart..	44	44	George Jones' Slaves.......	45	47
			Adam Cope		
69th District			Newton Plantation.......	15	15
John M. Cullens, Tr........	12	12			
Benjamin T. Edmund.......	5	5	*White Bluff District*		
			John Scriven's Slaves.......	47	47
CAMDEN COUNTY			James Pettegrew's Slaves....	63	63
W. Aldrich's Plantation.....	6	6	Dr. James Scriven's Slaves...	38	38
			James Hunter's Slaves......	101	106
CAMPBELL COUNTY.			Wm. Parker's Slaves.......	73	78
Philip Gatewood (Overseer)..	18	24	George Jones' Slaves.......	86	91
James T. Barnet (Overseer)..	35	36	William Law's Slaves.......	53	53
			Dr. Law's Slaves...........	35	35
CARROLL COUNTY			Estate of R. J. Houston.....	42	42
Zachariah Philips (family)...	14	14	Dr. Waring's Slaves........	69	70

GEORGIA—*Continued*

Name	Slaves	Total	Name	Slaves	Total
White Bluff District—Cont.			Wm. M. Roberts.		
George Glen's Slaves	25	25	overseer for Gen. Shorter	23	26
A. Barclay's Slaves	79	83			
T. Barton's Slaves	32	32	*30th Regiment Ga. Militia*		
Jno. H. Morel's Slaves	43	43	James Tyler overseer for		
Sampson Neyle's Slaves	36	36	Henry Cagler	29	31
John Millen's Slaves	21	21	Benjamin Garret overseer for		
Est. of Jno. Eppinger	28	28	Sam'l Reed	25	25
Jos. R. Gibsons	40	40	Blackman Dickson overseer		
Gabriel A. Moffett	7	7	for Capt. Barclay	9	10
			William Robey Executor of		
CLARKE COUNTY			Timothy Robey, Dec'd	7	11
Samuel Browne	15	15	Elizabeth Freeman Executor		
			of Jonah Freeman, Dec'd	2	10
COLUMBIA COUNTY					
Thos. Ware's Plantation	7	7	JONES COUNTY		
			Reynold Larkin	6	6
COWETA COUNTY					
M. Carrington, Guardian for			LIBERTY COUNTY		
the estate of J. Powell	19	22	Estate Adam Alexander dec'd.		
			By Alexander Stewart	39	39
DOOLY COUNTY			Estate William Anderson,		
Henry King	4	4	dec'd	63	70
			William P. Bowen	64	64
EFFINGHAM COUNTY			Elijah Baker for the Est. of		
Step. Tullas as manager of			John Lambert	67	69
Haig's Estate	40	40	Estate Joseph Bacon, Dec'd	28	31
Jeremiah Cuyler	72	72	Est. Thomas Baker dec'd	11	11
Paul Bevill	29	29	Est. Matthew Bennett	28	28
Hezekiah Ambrose	1	1	Alfred Cuthbert	31	31
Maria Patterson	8	8	Est. John Elliott, dec'd	117	117
			Martha Elliott	28	28
GLYNN COUNTY			Est. William Foster, dec'd	19	19
Isaac Abraham	5	5	Est. William Fleming, dec'd	34	34
Est. of Jas. Hamilton	229	229	Est. Daniel Fraser, dec'd	16	17
John Fraser	59	59	Est. Doc. R. H. Footman		
Daniel H. Braikford	59	59	dec'd	24	30
Samuel Moses and Chas.			Est. John E. Fraser, dec'd	9	10
Wright	15	15	Est. Palmer Goulden, dec'd	22	22
Est. Pierce Butler	270	270	Thomas Gould	17	17
Rosewell King, Jr.	44	44	Est. Joseph Hargroves dec'd	125	125
Est. E. Matthews	41	41	C. T. Hartt	15	15
Jos. Wiggins	8	8	George H. Johnston	133	138
John G. Bell	87	87	Agnes Middleton, agent St.		
John Burch	5	5	Catherines Island		
			James James	93	93
GUNNETT COUNTY			Est. Samuel Jones, dec'd	11	11
Geo. Stitt	9	9	Reuben King	26	26
			Barrington King by Thomas		
HOUSTON COUNTY			Dunham	72	73
Benjamin Farnell	2	2	Est. John Keel dec'd by		
			Capt. Wm. Maxwell	30	30
JACKSON COUNTY			Minors of Sam'l Lewis, dec'd	12	12
Theophilus Flowers' (Ne-			Est. James Lambright dec'd	12	13
groes)	4	5	Est. Col. Joseph Law dec'd		
			By Wm. M. W. Maxwell	55	59
JASPER COUNTY			Est. Sam'l Lewis Dec'd	47	47
38th Regiment and 1 company			Est. Robert E. McConnell	60	64
Lewis Dowdell's (Negroes)	11	12	Est. John Mallard, dec'd	24	25

GEORGIA—*Continued*

Name	Slaves	Total	Name	Slaves	Total
LIBERTY COUNTY—*Cont.*			*Capt. Hargroves District*		
Robert McIntosh..........	47	48	Wm. Winfrey for dec'd father	14	15
Est. James McCullough......	15	15			
Est. John McGowen........	3	3	*Capt. Haraiman's District*		
Sarah S. McGowen.........	3	3	Washington Hartsfield for		
John S. Mell for Est. William			father..................	31	45
Osgood dec'd............	54	57			
Susan M. Maxwell and			*Capt. Lampkin's District*		
Charles E. Jones.........	33	33	Little J. Brooke (Overseer J.		
Est. William Norman dec'd..	34	35	Phinizy)................	19	25
Est. Joseph Norman dec'd...	15	22	Moses Penn (Overseer J.		
Anney Powell by Silas Fulton	83	83	Phinizy)................	36	36
E. S. Reece..............	16	16			
Rev. James Shannon B......	15	15	*Capt. Walker's District*		
Est. James Stacy dec'd......	10	12	Daniel Rainey (Overseer for		
Est. Rev. C. O. Scriven....	77	82	B. Pope)...............	20	20
Est. Germin Fucker, dec'd...	6	6			
Est. John Way dec'd.......	36	42	*Capt. Hall's District*		
Jacob Wood..............	17	18	Wm. Walker, Ex. of W. Daw-		
			sey, dec'd..............	4	4
St. Catherine's Island					
Jacob Waldburg by Thomas			PULASKI COUNTY		
Oden, agent.............	85	85	*Capt. Stephen William's*		
Est. James Wilson dec'd....	9	9	*District*		
Est. John Winn, dec'd......	26	32	James M. Dunn's Plantation.	21	21
Est. William Ward, dec'd....	57	57			
Doc. Paul H. Wilkins, Jr....	22	22	PUTNAM COUNTY		
			Capt. John Kendrick's		
LINCOLN COUNTY			*District*		
Old Simon...............	7	7	William Whitehead's Plan-		
			tation..................	36	36
MONROE COUNTY					
James Thweatt (Slaves).....	56	56	*Late Capt. Thomas Wilkins'*		
			District		
MORGAN COUNTY			Nathan Lion's Plantation...	36	38
James Martin. O...........	3	4			
William Gaulding, O........	51	55	RICHMOND COUNTY		
James P. Butler, B. S. Jor-			*City of Augusta, First Ward*		
dan's Overseer...........	68	69	John T. Lamar's Slaves	2	3
John D. Timmonds. O.......	5	11	Mrs. Beall's Slaves.........	1	1
R. S. Hardways overseer.....	18	23	Mrs. Cantelous' Slaves......	6	6
			William Jackson's Slaves....	1	1
Capt. Kenzies 278			W. Pettis & Taliaferro's		
Samuel Ryland. (R. Taylor			slaves..................	2	2
overseer)...............	101	102	John Guimarin's Slaves.....	3	3
John G. Rieves (minor)......	25	26	W. W. Warren's Slaves......	6	6
			Mrs. Beall's Slaves.........	2	2
MUSCOGEE COUNTY			Mrs. Barrett's Slaves........	5	5
Buddy Bohannan..........	13	13	W. Brinn's Slaves..........	4	5
			Amelia Brigg's Slaves.......	4	4
Town of Columbus			Robert Dillin's Slaves.......	11	11
Benjamin Tarver..........	2	2	Dr. Baldwin's Slaves.......	4	4
			Isaac Taylor's Slaves.......	10	10
OGLETHORPE COUNTY			R. McCoomb's Slaves......	6	6
John Leales for R. Gordin..	26	27	Sarah Jones Slaves.........	2	2
Thomas C. Billips, overseer of			Wm. Rowland Slaves.......	1-	1
Baldwin, Wm., dec'd......	54	54	B. McKinnis' Slaves........	5	5

GEORGIA—*Continued*

Name	Slaves	Total	Name	Slaves	Total
City of Augusta, First Ward Cont.			P. Stovall's Slaves.........	1	1
			Juno Collins...............	3	3
H. Bowdris' Slaves.........	10	10	L. A. Riguil's Slaves........	11	11
John Hatfield and other Slaves..................	12	12	Susan William's Slaves......	5	5
			Samuel Hale's Slaves......	1	1
Mrs. Scott's Slaves.........	6	6	J. Andrews' Slaves..........	3	3
Mrs. Bacon's Slaves........	8	8	John P. King's Slaves......	5	5
			W. P. Deamond's Slaves....	4	4
Second Ward			Alexander Mackay's Slaves..	2	5
Charles Carter's Slaves.....	2	2	A. Waterman's Slaves.......	4	4
Mary Smelt's Slaves........	6	6	A. Gould's Slaves...........	6	6
Wm. McCray..............	3	3	John Fox's Slaves..........	4	4
Alfred Turpin's Slaves......	2	2	H. Bowdre's Slaves.........	5	5
Doctor Barny's Slaves......	3	3	B. H. Warren's Slaves......	4	4
Steam Boat Co's Slaves....	44	44	W. Moderwell's Slaves......	7	9
Jack Smith................	3	3	P. H. Mantz's Slaves......	3	3
Miss Garrett's Slaves.......	2	2	John P. King's Slaves.......	17	17
Beunly Walker's Slaves.....	2	2	G. A. B. Walker's Slaves....	2	2
Mrs. Mc Millan's Slaves.....	7	7	Thos. Flournoy's Slaves.....	2	2
Paul Rossignol's Slaves.....	8	15	H. Boudre's Slaves.........	5	5
R. R. Reid's Slaves........	4	4	S. Hale and Mrs. McKeen's slaves..................	4	4
Edward Thomas and other slaves	7	7	T. I. Walton's Slaves.......	6	6
			Mrs. Meredith's Slaves......	5	5
Third Ward			John Carrie's Slaves........	5	5
Peter Philpot..............	5	5	Miss Stalling's Slaves	11	12
Betsey Barnes.............	7	7	Paul Cottle's Slaves........	5	5
Julius Johnson.............	6	6	H. Bowdre's Slaves.........	4	4
R. H. Wilde's Slaves.......	5	5	John P. Greene's Slaves.....	5	10
Flora Kane...............	2	2	S. Bronson and Mrs. Clarke's Slaves.................	4	4
Alpha Oliver..............	8	8	D. Berry's Slaves..........	40?	42
Amy Barnes..............	4	4	John B. Given's Slaves......	2	3
E. F. Campbell's Slaves.....	9	9	Nelson Carter.............	34	34
James Harper's Slaves......	4	4			
Mrs. Fendall's Slaves.......	1	1	*Dunham District*		
H. Matthews' Slaves.......	3	3	Molly Brigg...............	2	2
H. Bowdus' Slaves.........	3	3	Jacob Hall................	8	8
Sarah McKinne............	4	3	William Shaunon...........	4	4
Billy Oliver..............	3	3	*Rhodes District*		
Winney Galphin...........	1	1	Samuel Dowse.............	7	7
Peter Fox.................	3	3			
Harry Phinizy.............	10	10	*Willcox District*		
Wm. Bostwick's Slaves.....	4	4	Samuel Hale...............	17	17
Frank Taylor's Slaves......	8	8	Hays Bowdre..............	7	7
William Harper's Slaves....	2	3			
Mrs. McCoy's Slaves.......	3	3	*Holt's District*		
A. Waterman's Slaves.......	1	1	Ann Milledge..............	16	16
E. Bacon's Slaves.........	7	7			
R. H. Musgrove's Slaves	5	6	SCREVEN COUNTY		
Mrs. Watkin's Slaves.......	3	3	*34th District*		
Aleck Pope...............	2	2	John Lovett...............	5	5
John Carmichael's Slaves ...	12	12			
Dennis Dent's Slaves.......	8	8	*38th District*		
Paul Rossignol's Slaves.....	6	6	Estate Telfare.............	56	57
Mrs. McMillan's Slaves.....	4	4			
Samuel Hale's Slaves.......	7	7	TROUP COUNTY		
Jonathan Meigs' Slaves.....	8	8	*Capt. John B. Strong*		
Eliza Ingraim's Slaves......	7	7	James W. Fanning's Quarter	19	19
Edward Thomas' Slaves....	6	6			

GEORGIA—*Continued*

Name	Slaves	Total	Name	Slaves	Total
WALTON COUNTY			John Burks..............	4	4
Nehemiah Gutry..........	3	3			
			167th District		
WARREN COUNTY			David Huff..............	21	21
Heirs of W. Andrews.......	6	6			
John M. Jackson (Overseer			*165th District*		
for Wm. Shivers).........	23	24	Elizabeth Hanson..........	23	23
Samuel Smith, Jr. and as over-			Mary A. Calloway.........	14	14
seer for Jos. Roberts......	16	20	Martha H. Calloway.......	11	11
R. S. Griggs (overseer for					
Thos. Berry).............	59	65	WILKINSON COUNTY		
			John Eady...............	9	9
WILKES COUNTY					
164th District					
Wm. B. Norman for Mrs. Pray	38	40			

KENTUCKY

Name	Slaves	Total	Name	Slaves	Total
ADAIR COUNTY			HENDERSON COUNTY		
Stephen McMillin..........	2	2	Craven Boswell, for the estate		
			of Newman Winsor.......	16	16
BOURBON COUNTY					
Robert Tallefarro..........	6	6	JEFFERSON COUNTY		
Z. Easton for Sam'l.......	5	5	J. D. Breckenridge........	17	17
Grace....................	2	2	John Hanes...............	17	17
James Smith..............	2	2	Elizabeth Brown...........	11	11
Tho. Y. Brent.............	6	6	Wm. Cooper..............	2	2
Mary Sodowsky...........	3	3			
			Town of Portland		
BRACKEN COUNTY			Louis Tariscon............	3	3
CAMPBELL COUNTY			*City of Louisville*		
Jno. W. Taliafero..........	10	10	Snead and Graham.........	44	44
			Wm. Cyrode..............	3	3
CLARKE COUNTY					
Anderson Col'd Sla........	2	2	JESSAMINE COUNTY		
			Charles Taylor of colour.....	4	4
FAYETTE COUNTY			Henry Taylor of colour......	8	8
Nancy Barr...............	8	8			
Elisha Warfield...........	11	11	LOGAN COUNTY		
Tom Graves..............	4	4	John W. Lacky............	23	23
Cuthbert Webb............	5	5			
Oliver Kenne.............	15	15	*Russellsville*		
William Challen............	2	2	Richard Curd.............	6	6
Joseph Ficklin............	9	9			
			MERCER COUNTY		
Lexington			Chas. Bosley.............	9	9
Gratz and Bruce...........	75	75	Chas. M. Cunningham......	2	2
Downing, Grand and Co....	9	9			
Tom Green................	3	3	NELSON COUNTY		
Cassell, Tilton and Cassell			Abram Gardiner...........	2	2
(Factory)................	37	37	John Caldwell.............	12	12
			Davy Samuels............	1	1
GARRARD COUNTY			Williby Beeler.............	2	2
John K. Withers...........	5	5	Benjamin Hardin..........	25	25
HARRISON COUNTY			*Bardstown*		
Brena Crosthwait..........	4	4	Mary McConcohe..........	9	9

KENTUCKY—*Continued*

Name	Slaves	Total	Name	Slaves	Total
Bardstown—Cont.			TODD COUNTY		
Daney Landsdale..........	1	1	Judith C. Scott............	1	1
John B. Wrighte...........	1	1	Richard Tunsdale..........	4	4
			Thomas McDougal........	11	11
SCOTT COUNTY					
Anthony Craig.............	2	2	UNION COUNTY		
			Edward Curry.............	13	13
SHELBY COUNTY			Robert Wimsatt ben taken...	3	3
South Side of Main Street					
in Shelbyville			WASHINGTON COUNTY		
Will. Rowland.............	6	6	Charles A. Wickliffe........	17	17
Widow Simerall............	2	2	H. & A. McElroy...........	11	11

LOUISIANA

Name	Slaves	Total	Name	Slaves	Total
ASCENSION PARISH			ST. LANDRY PARISH		
Rosétte Melançon..........	1	1	*Opelousas*		
			Manuel Laubre............	2	2
CONCORDIA PARISH			Jack Collins..............	4	4
David Latimore...........	7	7			
P. M. Lapiece.............	85	85	*Plaquemin Brulé*		
			Richard Andrus...........	6	6
E. FELICIANA PARISH			Henry Solomon............	13	13
El. W. Ripley..............	8	8			
			Bayou Téche		
IBERVILLE PARISH			Francois Corso............	1	1
Samuel Ogleton............	7	7	Baptiste B. Fontineau......	14	14
			Delphone B. Fontineau.....	3	3
JEFFERSON PARISH					
J. J. Mercier..............	3	3	*Grand Prairie*		
Vᵛᵉ. R. Avait..............	11	11	Dupré & Campbell........	8	8
LAFAYETTE PARISH			ST. MARTIN PARISH		
Veuve Eloy. Broupard dit			R. Francois Plantation......	26	26
Thboa.................	4	4	Oer. Delahoupage's Plannⁿ ...	70	70
			A. Abat's Plantation	36	41
New Orleans City			W. Moore's Plantation	20	21
Lebreton Deschapelle.......	3	3	M. G. Chretien Plantation ..	23	24
Lebaud..................	7	7	F. D. Conrad's Plantation ..	63	65
Jacob Eye................	1	1	Anteᵗᵉ. Dauterine	21	21
Jane Williams.............	2	2			
Cynthia Hyde.............	1	1	ST. MARYES PARISH		
Dr. Rice.................	7	7	Do. Do. (Following name of		
Thomas Brown............	1	1	A. Jackson)..............	13	13
			A. Frère Jr...............	28	28
POINT COUPEE			Miss Sophia Thomas.......	14	14
Benj. Poydras—estate of					
Point Coupee............	106	106	WASHITA (OUACHITA) PARISH		
G. Richard—estate of......	46	46	James Drew..............	4	4
Bennet Barrow—Point Cou-					
pee Estate..............	89	89	W. BATON ROUGE		
			Charles Bushnell's Negroes..	8	8
RAPIDES PARISH					
George G. Nelson..........	48	47	WEST FELECIANA PARISH		
George Mathews...........	108	108	Slaves of Taylor & Thornton	16	16
			John Smith's slaves and over-		
ST. BERNARD PARISH			seer...................	20	21
Joseph St. Amand.........	3	4	Ed. McGeeher's Slaves......	35	35

MARYLAND

Name	Slaves	Total	Name	Slaves	Total
ANNE ARUNDEL COUNTY			Catherine Beeks...........	4	4
Walter Smith..............	4	4	Jas. Carrol At McClair	22	24
Eliza Tydings.............	1	1	James Brown.............	2	2
Mrs. Stephenson...........	4	4			
Jno. Allen................	5	5	BALTIMORE COUNTY		
John Anderson............	5	5	*1st Collection District*		
Jno. S. Tyson.............	4	4	Bateman Dorsey..........	5	5
Thos. Snowden............	64	64	Benjamin Fuller..........	9	9
James Parker.............	7	7			
Charles Lucas............	9	9	*2nd Collection District*		
Charles Follen............	2	2	Jane Doore...............	1	1
Charles Carroll (of Carroll-			Elizabeth Hall............	7	7
ton)....................	307	307			
Edward W. Dorsey........	5	5	*3rd Collection District*		
Samuel Owings...........	6	6	James Smith.............	5	5
Philip H. Hopkins........	10	10			
Thomas Watkins..........	2	2	*4th Collection District*		
Archibald Edmonson.......	1	1	Acquilla Barnet...........	3	3
Richard Iglehart..........	2	2	Samuel Jones.............	2	2
Ruth Owings desert (?).....	9	9	William Patterson c.s.......	12	12
Andrew Dorsey...........	5	5	*Caroline Upper District No. 1*		
Walter C. Hammond.......	2	2	Levi Polter...............	10	10
			Samuel Blount.............	4	4
City of Annapolis			Hanah Morris.............	8	8
Ann Brummaid...........	1	1	James Henry.............	2	2
Susan Conner.............	5	5			
Dennis Diggs.............	3	3	CECIL COUNTY		
Jack Lyles................	4	4	*3rd Election District*		
Nelly Simms..............	4	4	Mingo Johnston...........	5	5
			William Stephenson........	1	1
City of Baltimore			Nannah Tillmon..........	4	4
1st Ward			Edward Johnson..........	2	2
Richd. Gough.............	3	3			
Jno. Williams.............	1	1	CHARLES COUNTY		
			Allens Fresh District		
2nd Ward			Elenor M. Digges.........	14	14
Hester Williams...........	2	2	Elizabeth Posey..........	6	6
Nathan Montgomery.......	9	9	William H. Smoot..........	8	8
Mariah Sprigs............	2	2	Sarrah E. Hanson.........	8	8
Tony Smith...............	2	2	Letty Maddox............	11	11
Perregrin Greenwood.......	3	3	Marshalls Quarter.........	26	26
Perry Talbot..............	5	5	Ann Vincent.............	9	9
Peter Clemmon...........	2	2	Elizabeth H. Newman......	4	4
David Murry.............	6	6	Doratha Boarman.........	18	18
William Gilbert...........	12	12	Fanny Redman...........	2	2
Paul Harmon..............	6	6	Phillip Barbes Quarters.....	22	22
George Hammond..........	3	3	Kitty Ross...............	1	1
			John R. Furguson.........	4	4
4th Ward			Nichls. Stamstreet Quarter..	20	20
Richard Emory............	2	2	James Howard............	1	1
			Lettey Harris............	11	11
5th Ward					
Charles Harrison..........	1	1	*3rd District (or Coomes)*		
			Harriet McPherson Quarter.	3	3
11th Ward			Charety Hanson Quarter....	6	6
William Brocton..........	2	2	Philip Stewart Quarter.....	70	70
			Jno. Rows. Heins.........	5	5
12th Ward			Jacob the property of Eliza-		
Phoebe Hanson...........	5	5	beth McPherson.........	1	1

MARYLAND—*Continued*

Name	Slaves	Total	Name	Slaves	Total
4th District (or Bryan Town)			Levin Thomas.............	3	3
Luke W. Barber...........	16	16	Daniel Jones..............	2	2
Phil Turner..............	8	8	Susan Giles..............	6	6
Jane Brent...............	4	4	Casandra Mooreland.......	1	1
Jane Watson..............	15	15	James Warren.............	3	3
			John Jones...............	1	1
Election District No. 2			Thomas Miles.............	3	3
New Market			Slaves belonging to Basil		
Sylvo. Simpson...........	4	4	Simpson & free persons		
Deborah Banks............	6	6	of Color................	4	6
Winnaher Pinder..........	13	13	John Lee (Slaves to Estate		
Rachel Mathews...........	4	4	of Stoner)...............	2	2
Jeffrey Henry............	2	2			
Alse Ranleigh............	1	1	*District 8*		
Cloe Washington..........	4	4	James Ogle...............	2	2
Kitty Green..............	4	4			
Nicy Bond...............	4	4	*District 6*		
Andrew Bryan.............	4	4	Benjamin Spriggs.........	5	5
			Black Sarah..............	2	2
Election District No. 3					
"Vienna"			HARFORD COUNTY		
Dinah Cephas.............	5	5	*District 2*		
Ritty Moluck.............	6	6	Richard D. Lee...........	7	7
Lavina Pattison..........	2	2	Abraham Jarrett..........	5	5
Harry Johnson...........	7	7			
Hager Jones..............	7	7	*District 3*		
Martha Griffith..........	3	3	Pheby Howard............	6	6
Delia Camper.............	5	5	Thomas Amos.............	5	5
Bill Gordon..............	2	2	Frank Taylor.............	2	2
Immanuel Harris..........	5	5			
Abram Waters.............	3	3	KENT COUNTY		
Lewis's Perry............	5	5	*District 1*		
Henny Banks.............	1	1	Pere Pearce..............	3	3
Mary Camper.............	8	8	James Mitchell...........	10	10
Martha Young............	4	4	Isaac Brice..............	5	5
Joe Hutson...............	5	5	Levi Murray.............	3	3
Hannah Young............	1	1	Harry Statin.............	5	5
Dinah Bayly.............	6	6	James Bowers............	23	23
Rhoda Owins.............	2	2	Benjamin Ringgold........	14	14
Ann Pinkett.............	3	3			
Priscilla Maulin.........	5	5	*District 3*		
			William Hackett..........	2	2
FREDERICK COUNTY			*Town of Millington*		
District 1			Nathaniel Grimes.........	1	1
Negro Lemuel.............	5	5			
Nancy Hillman............	6	6	*Georgetown X Roads*		
Henry Smith..............	3	3	Robert Worrell...........	1	1
Solomon Prout...........	10	10			
John Thomas..............	6	6	TALBOT COUNTY		
Jacob Hill...............	7	7	Henry Bush..............	2	2
James Green..............	4	4	Mary Cocer..............	3	3
			Delia Martin.............	3	3
District 3			Parris Webb..............	3	3
James Hollin.............	1	1	Nelly Rideout............	3	3
Godfrey Swan.............	5	5	Wm. Cuddy...............	2	2
William Goings...........	1	1			
			WASHINGTON COUNTY		
District 2			*District 6*		
John Bowen...............	3	3	Esther Briscoe...........	6	6

MARYLAND—*Continued*

Name	Slaves	Total	Name	Slaves	Total
Part of Hagerstown			Moses Norris	3	3
Catherine Butler	3	3	Isaac Harman	5	5
			Sarah Toadvine	4	4
WORCESTER COUNTY					
District 1			*District 3*		
John Robins	3	3	Rachel Johnson	5	5
			Comfort Ayres	10	10
District 2			Mary Purnell	2	2
Daniel Purnell	7	7	Allen Purnell	6	6
Peter Rackliffe	2	2			
Comfort Rackliffe	5	5	*Districts 4 and 5*		
Betty Purnell	2	2	Jacob Handy	2	2
			Leah Paremore	4	4
District 6			Jacob Mitchel	8	8
Samuel Turner	2	2	Peter Whaleys (Negroes)	23	23
Alpha Polk	6	6			

MISSISSIPPI

Name	Slaves	Total	Name	Slaves	Total
ADAMS COUNTY			LAWRENCE COUNTY		
City of Natchez			Charles Monroe	14	14
Mary F. Marton	11	11			
Walter Irvin	45	45	LOWNDES COUNTY		
Mrs. E. Greenfield	14	14	Samuel Garland	7	7
Griscilla Hoggot	17	17	Jane Stearne	12	12
John Pattason	34	34	Peter P. Pitchlyren	10	10
Egbert Sepious	8	8			
O. Lane	18	18	PERRY COUNTY		
			Peyton Chaney	6	6
CLAIBORNE COUNTY					
Thomas Farrar	6	6	SIMPSON COUNTY		
			Indian Nation attached to		
FRANKLIN COUNTY			*Simpson County*		
William Bell, Overseer of			Winny Battease	2	2
E. Turner	86	89	Benjamin Battease	2	2
Augustus Pitchford, Overseer			Jesse Bohannon	2	2
of Robert Anderson	38	40	Gen. Musaltubby	4	4
			John Wade	3	3
GREENE COUNTY			Lusony Harkins	14	14
Jesser Gwinn	3	3	George Turnbull	8	8
			Samuel Cobb	13	13
HANCOCK COUNTY			James Jones	1	1
John Joor	86	86	Solomon Jones	1	1
Jesse Cowan	8	8	James Pickens	1	1
			William Hayes	5	5
HINDS COUNTY			Queen Puxanubby	16	16
Jacin Carson	8	8	John Harris	3	3
Elisha Battle	32	32	Hayes Harrison	2	2
Patrick Henry	14	14			
Winter and Cockrell	7	7	WILKINSON COUNTY		
Benjamin Wilkins	51	51	Estate P. M. Green	38	38
JEFFERSON COUNTY			YAZOO COUNTY		
Moses Norman	2	2	Anthony Turnbull	4	4
			Wm. Leflore	2	2
JONES COUNTY			Vaugn Brashears	2	2
James Gardner	1	1			

MISSOURI

Name	Slaves	Total	Name	Slaves	Total
HOWARD COUNTY			St. Louis Township, City of St. Louis, Middle Ward		
Margaret (Temple) Tewple..	5	5	William Dellum...........	6	6
JEFFERSON COUNTY			Upper Ward, City of St. Louis		
Joachim Township			Lemuel Creed............	3	3
Isabella..................	1	1			
			Town of St. Genevieve		
ST. CHARLES COUNTY			Arcon (Negress)...........	2	2
Thomas L. Anderson.......	7	7	James Morison (Slaves).....	4	4
Russell Farnham...........	4	4			
Peter R. Beauchamp.......	5	5	SALINE COUNTY		
			Arrow Rock Township		
ST. LOUIS COUNTY			Fleming Marshall, overseer..	9	10
Jefferson Barracks, "6th Reg't"			WASHINGTON COUNTY		
			Richwood Township		
Coln Baker...............	1	1	John Griffin..............	5	5

NEW JERSEY

Name	Slaves	Total	Name	Slaves	Total
BURLINGTON COUNTY			MONMOUTH COUNTY		
Township of Nottingham			Freehold		
Stephin Duwer (?).........	2	2	Thomas Barcalow.........	1	1
Stephen Seaberry..........	2	2			
James Lenox..............	2	2			

NORTH CAROLINA

Name	Slaves	Total	Name	Slaves	Total
ANSON COUNTY			George P. Devereux........	19	19
Henry W. Harrington	34	34	John Devereux............	204	204
Estate of Chapman........	25	25	Whitmell Rutland..........	7	7
Estate of Wm. Marshall	25	25	Noah H. Thompson........	43	43
Malicha Peques...........	20	20	William D. Louther........	23	23
			William M. Clark.........	129	129
BEAUFORT COUNTY			Joseph J. Williams.........	24	24
Washington			Samuel Peter.............	1	1
Wm. Bernard.............	3	3	Violet...................	1	1
Wm. Armstrong...........	4	4	David Williams...........	13	13
Wm. McPheters...........	4	4	Lewis Williams...........	72	72
Joshua Taylor.............	2	2			
Coleman Heirs.............	7	7	BLADEN COUNTY		
Jarvis B. Buxton...........	8	8	Maurice Waddel..........	7	7
			Edmund B. Waddel........	7	7
Beaver Dam			Wellington Waddel.........	13	13
John G. Blount............	3	3	Hugh Waddel.............	1	1
			Arthur Hill..............	1	1
South Creek			Martha Lucas.............	1	1
Wm. Hill.................	2	2	Richard Parish............	4	4
			James Owen..............	33	33
BERTIE COUNTY			Lunnun Wallace...........	9	9
John Green..............	18	18			
Jamy B. Urquhart........	18	18	BRUNSWICK COUNTY		
Thomas B. Thompson......	38	38	John Swann..............	65	65
Samuel Williams..........	56	56	William B. Meares (?)......	51	51
Whitmill Pregh............	12	12	John Walker.............	37	37
William T. Thompson......	73	73	Caroline Eagles............	25	25
John Granburey...........	14	14	Maurin Waddle Jr..........	13	13
Robert A. Jones...........	132	132	Thos. Cowan..............	82	82

NORTH CAROLINA—*Continued*

Name	Slaves	Total	Name	Slaves	Total
Camden County			Cufee (?) Barnard..........	8	8
Peter McBride...........	7	7			
			Davidson County		
Carteret County			Peter Harstons Quarter.....	24	24
Portsmouth Dist.			J. Hargraves Est. by Baily...	38	38
John G. Blunt............	3	3			
			Edgecomb County		
Caswell County			*District No. 2*		
Romulus M. Sanders.......	4	4	James Battle's Slaves.......	227	227
William J. Nash...........	4	4			
William Bethell...........	7	7	*District No. 4*		
Holoway Pass.............	7	7	Henry J. G. Ruffin's Slaves...	5	5
Eustace Hunt.............	17	17			
Roger Atkinson (Estate)....	17	17	*District No. 16*		
Jesse Carter Doct;.........	4	4	Willie Burn's Slaves........	10	10
Chatham County			**Franklin County**		
William Hayes Estate......	17	17	*Perrie's District*		
Maman (?) Moore..........	13	13	Macklin's Essex (?).........	2	2
Alexander D. Moore........	2	2			
Susan Hill................	3	3	*Foster's District*		
Nathanl. Hill.............	2	2	Brodie's Essex (?)	8	8
			Brodie's David.............	8	8
Chowan County					
William Wright Va. (?).....	25	25	*Gill's District*		
			Taylor's Zelus.............	10	10
Craven County			Taylor's Elisha............	7	7
Michael Fisher............	4	4			
George Bryan..............	25	25	**Gates County**		
John F. Smith.............	30	30	Taylor Robin..............	2	2
John B. Smith.............	2	2	James Williams............	8	8
Henry Black..............	17	17	Whitmier Stallings (Fr. D.		
Joseph Mares..............	5	5	Outlaw?)................	33	33
John L. Durand...........	7	7	Edwin Copeland...........	31	31
John R. Donnell...........	25	25			
			Granville County		
Newbern North Side of Neuse			*North Regiment*		
River			William A. Somerville.......	15	15
William Dunkin...........	6	6	Horace T. Royster.........	26	26
Jane Tilman..............	17	17	Isabella Jeffreys...........	3	3
John W. Guion............	20	20			
			South Regiment		
Cumberland County			J. A. Downey Plt..........	19	19
Town of Fayetteville					
John Waddill..............	3	3	*Beaver Dam District*		
Duncan Campbell adm......	4	4	John Green Plt.............	24	24
David Smith Negroes.......	13	13	Reyks & Southerland.......	2	2
Neil McKethan Negroes....	4	4			
Ann Williams Do..........	4	4	*Fort Creek District*		
Frederick Miller do........	5	5	Robert Taylor Plt..........	23	23
Sarah Thomas do	4	4			
Joel Williams (Trustee).....	4	4	*Epping Forest*		
R. T. Goodwin (Admin.)....	1	1	John Ealon Plt.............	47	47
Joseph Baker (Agent).......	16	16	Doct. Hawkins Plt..........	19	19
W. Lord's (Negroes)........	5	5			
T. C. Hooper (Negroes).....	5	5	*Henderson District*		
			Wm. Robard Col...........	21	21
Currituck County			Phillip Hawkins Col........	1	1
Daniel Wilson.............	4	4			

NORTH CAROLINA—*Continued*

Name	Slaves	Total	Name	Slaves	Total
HALIFAX COUNTY			Thomas Weathersbee........	1	1
A. R. Govan..............	1	1	Kenneth Hyman..........	7	7
Mary Pugh................	1	1			
Cadwallader Jones..........	28	28	**MECKLENBURG COUNTY**		
William Williams..........	24	24	Eli Springs................	22	22
Bartholomew Barrow.......	19	19	Doct. William J. Polk.......	67	67
Sarah Coffield.............	7	7	Genl. Thomas G. Polk......	33	33
John T. Johnson...........	33	33	John M. Pourter (So. Car.)..	12	12
Charity Barns.............	46	46			
William Williams..........	61	61	**NASH**		
Susan Plummer............	25	25	*District No. 5—Basses*		
James Biggs...............	10	10	Spencer Alston............	13	13
James B. Urquhart.........	18	18			
			NEW HANOVER COUNTY		
HARTFORD COUNTY			William Picket............	5	5
Amos Rainer..............	7	7	W. Lazarus................	30	30
William Clinton...........	17	17	William H. Beaty..........	39	39
Jacob Menfee..............	2	2	Joshua James.............	9	9
David Jinkins.............	2	2	F. J. Swan.................	55	55
Sesar Copeland............	2	2	Jno. D. Toomer............	35	35
			Wm. Lord Exr. of G. H.		
HYDE COUNTY			Walker Estate...........	37	37
At Clark's................	6	6	Mrs. A. Hill..............	20	20
Clark's Mill..............	3	3	Col. S. Ashe..............	70	70
			Mrs. Moore...............	14	14
IREDELL COUNTY			Josh James...............	20	20
Thomas Byers.............	8	8	Richard Bradley...........	20	20
John Graham..............	11	11	Robt. Cowan..............	39	39
Henry W. Connor..........	16	16	Thos. C. Reston............	38	38
Milus Doblims.............	1	1	R. Edens.................	13	13
Enoch Erwin..............	12	12	John W. Livingston........	6	6
John Wood................	2	2	Alexander Miller...........	23	23
Etheldrid Edwards.........	5	5	William W. Jones..........	29	29
Isaac Green Sen...........	7	7	Gusken Lazarus...........	5	5
Jeremiah Gaither..........	8	8	Joseph Gorrie.............	10	10
Greenberry Gaither........	3	3			
Elam Gaither..............	4	4	**NORTHAMPTON COUNTY**		
Eli Harris................	5	5	Mungo T. Ponton..........	7	7
Alvin Howard.............	1	1	Robert A. Jones...........	19	19
Lazarus Holman...........	15	15	James Gee.................	22	22
James H. Hall............	12	12	William Clarke............	39	39
James Holmes.............	1	1	Littleberry Mason.........	39	39
Isaac Green Jun...........	1	1	Benjamin Williamson.......	7	7
Josiah Johnston...........	2	2	Benjamin Lashley..........	10	10
Amos Lovelace............	2	2	Matthew Harrison.........	14	14
			Thomas Bracy.............	11	11
JOHNSTON COUNTY			Robert H. Wilson.........	74	74
William B. Allen..........	1	1	Mary Jones...............	7	7
David....................	47	47			
Abram...................	6	6	**ORANGE COUNTY**		
John.....................	7	7	Kirkland & Wall...........	4	4
Squire...................	3	3	Susannah Faucett.........	10?	11
LENOIR COUNTY			**PASQUOTANK COUNTY**		
Nathan Lauter............	6	6	Caleb Perkins.............	6	6
			James C. Johnson..........	100	100
MARTIN COUNTY					
Henry Mitchell...........	5	5	**PERQUIMANS COUNTY**		
Thomas Pugh.............	4	4	James Miller..............	2	2

NORTH CAROLINA—*Continued*

Name	Slaves	Total	Name	Slaves	Total
PERQUIMENS CO.—*Cont.*			Aspasio Earle, Agent.......	12	12
Hugh K. Wyatt...........	2	2	Winny Brooks.............	4	4
Exum Elliott..............	4	4	Samuel Jenkins, Agent......	12	12
PERSON COUNTY			SAMPSON COUNTY		
David Pointer.............	11	11	James Williamson..........	5	5
John Brooks...............	8	8			
Green Wisdon.............	3	3	SURRY COUNTY		
Joseph Armstrong..........	6	6	Richard C. Puryear........	15	15
			Thomas Conrad's Estate....	4	4
PITT COUNTY					
John Jones................	2	2	WAKE COUNTY		
			Sarah (of Clendenings est.)..	1	1
RICHMOND COUNTY					
Steele's District			*Raleigh*		
Duncan McRae (of Mont-			Theophilus Hunter.........	2	2
gomery)................	1	1	Beverly Daniel............	5	6
Mial Covington (Overseer					
Leaks Estate)	37	37	*Buffaloe District*		
			Drury Morgan.............	3	3
Fair Ground District			William Bush..............	4	4
Charles Robinson Guardian			Stephen Bell..............	2	2
for Thos. Robinson.......	5	5	Nathaniel Perry............	5	5
Stewart's District			*Marks Creek District*		
Angus Fairby (of Robeson			Sarah Stone...............	41	41
County)................	7	7			
			St. Maries District		
Williamson's District			Ephraim Andrews..........	3	3
Town of Rockingham			Commons Luke............	4	4
William Crawford (Shff ?)...	1	1	B. S. King................	2	2
			William H. Haywood Sen....	3	3
ROBESON COUNTY			Delia Haywood............	9	9
John Odeneal..............	8	8	Elenor Haywood...........	38	38
			Alford Haywood...........	7	7
ROCKINGHAM COUNTY			Elizabeth Filton (?)	8	8
Wm. Allen (Overseer for R.			Simmons J. Baker..........	17	17
M.)...................	11	11	John Stuart...............	5	5
Nathaniel Shields..........	4	4	Anna White...............	16	16
Robert Dalton.............	4	4	Abraham Bracie...........	2	2
ROWAN COUNTY			*St. Matthew's District*		
M. Chambers' Negroes......	14	15	Nath'l. Spears (Oversr. for		
Hartsall's Negroes.........	3	3	Col. Polk)..............	14	14
James Martin's Plantation...	52	52	William H. Haywood Jr.....	4	4
Mrs. Henderson's Plantation.	79	79	Henry M. Miller (Joy Peter-		
Brown, Michael's Plantation	37	37	son Oversr.).............	11	11
Jas. Huie's Plantation	71	71	Wm. Henry Haywood Senr..	27	27
			Allen Haywood............	5	5
Town of Salisbury			Ths. D. Bennaham.........	35	35
John L. Henderson........	2	2	Ann Cameron.............	44	44
			Abraham Reucher.........	7	7
RUTHERFORD COUNTY					
Hamelton Mary...........	13	13	*Raleigh W. of Halifax & Fay-*		
John Logan...............	16	16	*etteville Sts.*		
John McEntire.............	19	19	George E. Badger..........	2	2
John Shields..............	9	9	Benj. A. Barham..........	1	1
Peter Summey.............	3	3			

NORTH CAROLINA—*Continued*

Name	Slaves	Total	Name	Slaves	Total
WARREN COUNTY			Rebecca Hill..............	4	4
Nutbush District					
Henry Woodworth..........	3	3	WAYNE COUNTY		
Wm. Hendrick.............	7	7	Richard B. Hatch..........	28	28
Hawtree District			WILKES COUNTY		
Drewry Gill..............	32	32	Elizabeth Horton..........	5	5
River District			*Abbeville*		
Rebecca Carroll............	14	14	Henry Reede..............	9	9
			Hutson Brinel.............	6	6
Fishing Creek District			Diner Vickery.............	6	6
Sally Dawson..............	5	5	John C. Calhoun...........	34	34
			The Estate of T. Lipscomb...	28	28
Shocco District			John Marshall.............	10	10
Richard Hines.............	2	2			

SOUTH CAROLINA

Name	Slaves	Total	Name	Slaves	Total
ANDERSON COUNTY			Thomas P. Fripp...........	31	31
Thomas Blassingame (Resident in Pickens) Slaves in Anderson..............	9	9	Miss Ffirth................	9	9
			Elizabeth Graham..........	3	3
			Esta. Joseph Greive........	9	9
David Moore (Resident in Spartanburgh) Slaves in Anderson..............	8	8	William Joyner............	4	4
			Esta. Mary Jenkins.........	43	43
			Esta. John Jenkins.........	2	2
Samuel Warren (Resident in Charleston District) Slaves in Anderson.............	28	28	Charles M. Myers..........	13	13
			Esta. Adam Perryclear......	19	19
Horatio Reese (Resident in Pickens) Slaves in Anderson	17	17	Arthur G. Rose............	21	21
			Ann Reynolds..............	54	54
			Esta. Edwd. Reynolds......	4	4
Pickens District			Esta. John Rhodes.........	45	45
John C. Calhoun (?)........	37	37	Esta. Henry Richardson.....	35	35
Robert Hacket.............	·8	8	Esta. Benj. D. Scott........	33	33
Elizabeth Sloan...........	12	12	Esta. John Shorten.........	4	4
Robert Maxwell...........	19	19	John Stapleton Colo........	160	160
			Revd. Jos. Wallace.........	22	22
Barnwell			Abm. Eustis Colo..........	84	84
Alexander Tilfair...........	48	48	Esta. Jno. O. Prentiss.......	43	43
B. P. & O. Cohen..........	3	3			
Michael Brown............	15	15	*St. Luke's Parish*		
Thos. G. Lamar...........	9	9	William Barnwell..........	46	49
C. N. Northrop............	26	28	Esta. Arthur F. Behn.......	16	16
			Esta. Henry Bona.........	17	17
BEAUFORT COUNTY			James Campbell...........	28	28
St. Helena Parish			Jacob D. Guerard..........	42	42
Willm. H. Barnwell.........	34	34	John B. Grimball..........	49	49
Esta. Thomas Bell.........	36	36	Mrs. Wilson Glover........	148	148
Esta. Ann Boucher.........	15	15	John H. Glover............	92	302
Esta. Archd. Campbell......	25	25	Esta. Thomas Heyward.....	147	147
Esta. Saxby Chaplin........	49	49	Henry J. Hartstene........	18	18
Esta Edward Cuthbert......	50	50	James E. McPherson.......	46	46
Esta. Mary Coffin..........	163	163	Esta. Phillip Matthews.....	18	18
Miss M. B. Elliott.........	74	74	Mary P. Pope.............	49	54
Stephen Elliott.............	50	50	Mrs. James Stoney.........	17	17
W. & B. Edings............	61	61	Esta. James Stoney........	196	196
Esta. Paul Fripp...........	28	28	George M. Stoney.........	112	112
			Thomas M. Smith..........	28	28

SOUTH CAROLINA—*Continued*

Name	Slaves	Total	Name	Slaves	Total
St. Peter's Parish			Berkeley County		
Michael Brown............	45	45	*Saint James Goose Creek*		
Esta. Sarah Brooks.........	7	7	Isaih Moses...............	35	35
Jane & Sisters Bourke.......	9	9	Est. Dr. Irving..........	81	81
Mary Ferguson............	9	9	Isham Schuler............	15	15
Esta. T. V. Gray...........	6	6	Revd. M. Pogson..........	40	40
Esta. Js. Hardee Senr.......	6	6	Berlingham Rudd.........	15	15
Esta. Willm. Hardee........	9	9	Dr. John Wilson..........	133	133
Esta. Isaac Hardee Junr.....	16	16	Thomas Schriven..........	95	95
Mary Kelly...............	5	5	Mrs. Press Smith.........	70	70
Esta. Willm. Lawton.......	77	77	H. M. Smith.............	20	20
John Middleton...........	5	5	Est. Mrs. Nesbit.........	20	20
Mary Myers..............	5	5	Est. Wm. Platt..........	10	10
John D. Mongin...........	33	33	Walter Izard.............	105	105
Esta. John Patterson.......	6	6	M. Keckely..............	42	42
James P. Screven..........	62	62	P. & M. Lesesne..........	28	28
Archibald Smith...........	57	57	Est. E. Luton............	20	20
Esta. Archd. Smith........	36	36	Est. R. Mathews.........	80	80
Richd. & F. Williams.......	18	18	Est. W. Liston...........	106	106
Daniel E. Huger...........	200	200	Est. James Harvey........	7	7
Esta. Willm. Heyward......	87	87	Est. Hamilton Hart.......	10	10
Willm. Heyward Junr.......	11	11	Isaac Conner.............	18	18
William C. Daniels........	116	116	Est. J. Dehay............	43	43
			J. Langstaff.............	20	20
Prince Williams Parish			Henry Smith.............	65	65
Robert W. Barnwell.......	77	77	John Hanahan...........	7	7
Edward Barnwell..........	71	71	E. H. Edwards...........	25	25
Esta. Nathl. Barnwell......	55	55	Dr. E. Brailsford.........	2	2
Willm. H. Barnwell.......	18	18	Joseph Manigault........	12	12
Esta. John G. Barnwell.....	45	45	George Chisohn (?)........	65	65
Miss Charlotte Bull........	40	40	Honorable Wm. Johnson....	26	26
Lucius Cuthbert..........	34	34	C. Winthrop..............	58	58
George Chisolm Junr.......	68	68	John Parker.............	50	50
Martha Chaplin...........	42	42	C. K. Lesesne...........	13	13
Stephen Elliott...........	22	22	Mrs. J. Gadsden.........	58	58
Edgar Tripp..............	33	33	T. H. Deas..............	45	45
John Guerard............	4	4	Est. Geo. Robertson.......	58	58
Saml. R. Gillison..........	124	126	C. F. Brown.............	27	27
Thomas S. Gillison........	69	69	F. L. Curtis.............	8	8
Nathl. Heyward...........	15	15	J. L. Glenn.............	18	18
Isaac R. Jenkins..........	68	68	M. E. Logan.............	17	17
John La'Roche...........	29	29	Dr. C. Dezel............	32	32
Esta. John Law...........	13	13	Charles Graves...........	62	62
Elvira McPherson.........	24	24	Barnard E. Bee..........	48	48
Esta. John McLeod........	24	24	J. L. Postell............	8	8
Mrs. Matthews (of St. Andrews).................	16	16	*Saint Andrews*		
John Milne..............	37	37	Samuel Prioleau..........	5	5
Samuel Reed.............	60	60	E. Bellinger.............	10	10
Mary B. Stuart...........	74	74	C. Williman.............	22	22
Henry M. Stuart..........	24	24	William Bell.............	26	26
Middleton Stuart.........	57	57	James McDonald.........	48	48
Willm. Smith (son James)...	18	18	David D. Cohen..........	23	23
Thomas Talbird..........	62	62	C. Williman.............	14	14
Esta. John R. Toomer......	30	30	Edward Jones............	10	10
Esta. Henry Toomer.......	6	6	Mordecai Cohen..........	27	27
Esta. Edwd. Neufville......	26	26	William Brisbane..........	35	35

SOUTH CAROLINA—*Continued*

Name	Slaves	Total	Name	Slaves	Total
Saint Andrews—Cont.			George A. Hazlehurst.......	27	27
Charles Drayton...........	33	33	John Johnson..............	7	7
Frederick Touchstone.......	13	13	Mary Lord................	5	5
John Hume................	23	23	Thomas Mitchell..........	22	22
Barnard E. Bee............	19	19			
Henry O Hara.............	7	7	*Christ Church*		
William Cattell...........	38	38	Richard Allen.............	6	6
R. Lining.................	23	23	Brandt...................	1	1
S. L. Simons..............	69	69	Bowman..................	9	9
J. J. Pringle..............	88	88	A. H. McGillivray.........	4	4
T. B. Seabrook............	74	74	William Matthews.........	41	41
T. H. Deas	46	46	R. T. Morrison...........	40	40
H. B. Crafts..............	42	42	Joseph Manigault..........	7	7
Joseph Cole..............	16	16	William Pritchard.........	9	9
Elias Horry...............	43	43	William Price.............	49	49
C. Hanckell..............	25	25	Pickens..................	35	35
James O Hear.............	57	57	William Smith............	3	3
William Mathews.........	20	20			
John Limbecker...........	8	8	*St. James Santee*		
Jos. B. Rivers............	28	28	Theo. Gourdin Est.........	49	49
Gilbert C. Geddes.........	10	10	William Hume............	4	4
Robt. J. Turnbull.........	42	42	John B. Lynch............	64	64
C. Staley................	50	50	William Lucas...........	44	44
Joseph Bee..............	28	28	Joseph Manigaulte.........	13	13
C. C. Smith..............	10	10	Saml. H. Mortimer.........	53	53
James Murray............	7	7	Fanny Pinckney...........	82	82
Benjn. Fuller............	78	78	H. P. Rutledge............	23	23
Thomas Wigfall..........	38	38	James Shoolbread.........	6	6
Paul C. Grimball..........	48	48	C. J. Steedman...........	3	3
James Magwood..........	39	39	Philip Tidyman...........	4	4
Joseph Seabrook..........	42	42			
Benjamin Roper...........	49	49	*Judicial District of Geo. Town*		
J. S. Gibbes..............	38	38	F. M. Barnet.............	60	60
L. Browning..............	19	19	Elizabeth Cheesborough.....	6	6
A. Middleton.............	153	153	Mrs. Harel...............	28	28
Andrew Milne	18	18	Robert Lester.............	34	34
Benjamin Elliott..........	8	8			
			City of Charleston		
St. John's Berkley			*Ward No. 1*		
Blacklock	6	6	George Chisolm Junr.......	4	4
Wm. Blamyer.............	3	3	Robert Russell...........	7	7
James Ferguson...........	99	99	Minde Righton...........	8	8
Theo. Gourdin Est.........	4	4	Mary Ann Derritt.........	7	7
			Sarah Wagner.............	4	4
Saint Stephen's			Bella Parker..............	37	37
Stephen Herren...........	8	8	Hannah Hussey...........	4	4
Ann Lehre................	34	34	Louisa Connolley..........	3	3
Francis Peyre Est..........	30	30	P. Weston................	15	15
William Sinkler...........	10	10	Katey Drayton:	25	25
St. Thomas & St. Dennis			*Ward No. 2*		
Thomas Bonneau..........	3	3	Charlotte Rose...........	12	12
Wm. G. Brown...........	55	55	Clarissa Hasell...........	7	7
Henry Cannady...........	11	11	Susan Douglass...........	8	8
Catharine Edwards........	73	73	Herriott Ashe.............	4	4
George Elfe Est...........	12	12	Sukey Dupont.............	25	25
John Glenn...............	9	9	Fanny Furman............	15	15
John L. Geyer............	12	12	Sarah Holmes.............	17	17

SOUTH CAROLINA—*Continued*

Name	Slaves	Total	Name	Slaves	Total
Ward No. 2—Cont.			Sylvia Irving............	7	7
Sally Holmes.............	8	8	Sylvia Jones.............	9	9
Prince Bee...............	15	15	Fanny Boyd..............	4	4
Ann Jones...............	10	10	Juno Waller.............	31	31
Frances Prior............	4	4	Flora Dawson............	3	3
Jane Middleton...........	10	10	Phoebe Lee.............	4	4
Amaretta Cox............	8	8	Betty Kennedy...........	10	10
Thomas & Henry Grimke....	6	6	Elizabeth Wood..........	14	14
Sifley & Mentzing.........	16	16	Philis Aiken.............	7	7
			C. Chitty................	3	3
Ward No. 3			Phillis Fields...........	3	3
Grace Muggridge.........	13	13	John & Henry Horlbeck.....	38	38
Beck Moett..............	10	10	Fanny Graham...........	5	5
Rose Dobson.............	9	9	Jane Wilson.............	6	6
Rose Wigfall.............	3	3	Sophia Moncrieffe........	3	3
Mary Lewis..............	8	8	Jane Jones...............	5	5
Mary Ann Elfe...........	16	16	Hannah Mitchell..........	14	14
Mary Salvo..............	7	7	Maria Lopez.............	6	6
York Lessesue...........	13	13	Rachel Myers............	10	10
Diana McCready..........	5	5	Peter Motta.............	9	9
Patrick Caldwell.........	15	15	Nelly Forrest............	4	4
Catherine Brisson.........	6	6	Reuben Bell.............	6	6
Nancy Ashe.............	9	9	Nancy Deas.............	2	2
Patience Burns...........	59	59	Miley Wragg.............	6	6
Rose McCready..........	9	9	Diana Wagner...........	1	1
Hannah Cochran..........	5	5	Jane Campbell...........	4	4
Peggy Pinckney..........	5	5	Amelia Mathews..........	4	4
Bynah Toomer...........	3	3	Mary Oajer..............	8	8
Nelly Smith.............	10	10	Hetty Moses.............	5	5
Sally Black..............	11	11	Harriott Lewis...........	9	9
Rose Fraser.............	11	11	Nancy Hart.............	16	16
Mary Bull...............	10	10	Est. I Bellenger..........	12	12
Emma Bryan.............	5	5	Nancy Middleton.........	6	6
Lucy Smith..............	10	10	Emma Dumont...........	7	7
Jane Nicholson...........	3	3	Miley Harris.............	8	8
Eliza DeVillers....	4	4	Amey Hurst.............	7	7
Matilda Parker...........	4	4	Phillis Elfe.............	9	9
Sarah Pritchard..........	7	7	Nancy Evans.............	6	6
Nancy Jenner (?)..........	3	3	Nancy Bell.............	14	14
Sarah Legare............	2	2	March Bennett...........	7	7
Rachel Dupre............	2	2	Nancy North.............	6	6
Sylvia Bull..............	2	2	Joe Read................	4	4
Cyrus Little.............	8	8	Aaron Green.............	13	13
Patty Olin..............	24	24	Paul Wilkie.............	11	11
Bella Moultrie...........	2	2	Peter Bennett............	15	15
Bella Perry.............	6	6	Lewis Horry.............	4	4
Sylvie Birnie............	7	7	Mary Wilson.............	3	3
Hagar Walker...........	12	12	Lucy Clarke.............	7	7
Dinah Smith.............	12	12			
Eliza Hence.............	7	7	*Charleston Neck*		
Sarah Keenan............	10	10	Grace Mitchell...........	12	12
Mary Nervon............	6	6	Nelly Butler.............	11	11
Thomas Gadsden..........	6	6	Betty Maxwell...........	8	8
			Richard Snow...........	8	8
Ward No. 4			Emma Yates.............	10	10
Beck Strap..............	24	24	Louisa Jones.............	13	13
Chloe Miller.............	14	14	Ellen Deseisseline.........	7	7
James Shepherd..........	3	3	Mary Michel.............	9	9

SOUTH CAROLINA—*Continued*

Name	Slaves	Total	Name	Slaves	Total
Charleston Neck—Cont.			Thomas Oliver..............	9	9
John M. Van Rhyn........	14	14	Archey Lord...............	11	11
Chloe Perry.............	11	11	J. Payn's Garden...........	9	9
Jemmy Dawson.............	12	12	Daniel Blake...............	17	17
Thomas Cox...............	6	6	R. R. Gibbes..............	14	14
Chloe Michel.............	13	13	Thomas D. Condy.........	12	12
Henry Fogartie...........	6	6	George W. Cross...........	13	13
Charlotte Maverick........	8	8	D. Dezel..................	12	12
Pussey Belser.............	7	7	C. Muckenfuss.............	11	11
Mary Discon.............	12	12	James L. Gibbes...........	13	13
Charlotte Simms...........	9	9	Jacob Martin..............	15	15
John Mordecai............	11	11	W. Bailey.................	10	10
Prince Jacobs.............	4	4			
Phillis Forris.............	11	11	CHESTER COUNTY		
Cate Hernandez...........	11	11	B. Fetherston............	2	2
James Washington........	12	12			
Cate Hume...............	9	9	*Chesterfield*		
Willis Wilson.............	13	13	Hezekiah Hough...........	2	2
Maurice Harris...........	5	5	Peter Kelly...............	2	2
Polly Carson.............	6	6	Jno. K. McIver...........	1	1
Tisby Wright..............	8	8	Jos. H. Towns.............	3	3
Diana Geddes.............	10	10			
Sambo Robinson...........	4	4	COLLETON COUNTY		
L. McCall.................	7	7	*St. Bartholomews Parish*		
James Gadsdens (farm).....	14	14	Benjn. Bythewood........	52	52
H. S. Waring "	3	3	Elizabeth Ulmer..........	7	7
Cole Cattell "	11	11	B. C. Fishburn............	8	8
John Pratt's (farm)........	6	6	Sophia Skining.............	163	163
A. G. Rose "	10	10	William Walter............	11	11
John Horlbeck (farm)......	21	21	Josiah Taylor..............	14	14
Jacob Dela Motta..........	4	4	L. P. Gough (Esta.)........	69	69
James Perry...............	11	11	Sophia Shepherd...........	54	54
William Sanders...........	12	12	F. Benjamin Hard........	10	10
Stephen Elliott...........	13	13	Benja. B. Smith (Esta.).....	42	42
John Glen.................	7	7	John Trescott Est..........	48	48
John Magrath..............	11	11	Ann. A. Hutchinson........	89	89
Thomas Cochran...........	5	5	Paul S. H. Lee............	52	52
M. Faber.................	15	15	M. H. Neyle................	77	77
Charles Carrier...........	8	8	Maurice Simmons..........	19	19
Loughton Smith...........	10	10	Philip Costell..............	36	36
H. C. Plover.............	23	23	Nathanl. G. Clary.........	69	69
Nicholas Cobia............	25	25	M. E. Baynard............	53	53
John Fraser...............	21	21	Mrs. McPherson...........	7	7
John Shoolbread	13	13	R. Thomas Smith.........	74	74
Joseph Johnson...........	6	6	Wm. Lowndes	65	65
Harry Edwards...........	6	6	Ann Pringle...............	59	59
James F. Edwards.........	9	9			
N. Heyward (2 places)......	106	106	*St. Paul's Parish*		
Benjamin Markley.........	10	10	Sophia Shepherd...........	2	2
Theodore Gaillard.........	11	11	Esta. Joseph A. Smith......	54	54
Robert Gibbes.............	17	17	Peter T. Merchant.........	4	4
J. Lucas (Farm)...........	5	5	John G. Schutt.............	81	81
Richard Yeadow...........	13	13	John B. Vaughan..........	48	48
William Lowndes..........	23	23	Wm. W. Ancrum...........	112	112
George Cox...............	26	26	Alex. England.............	82	82
Richard Cunningham.......	5	5	Wm. Fox..................	33	33
George Johnston...........	4	4	J. E. McPherson...........	51	52
Jos. Turpin..............	5	5	Sarah E. Waring...........	37	37

SOUTH CAROLINA—*Continued*

Name	Slaves	Total	Name	Slaves	Total
St. Paul's Parish—Cont.			KERSHAW COUNTY		
W. G. Logan..............	23	23	H. Abbott Est.............	2	2
Wm. Washington Est.......	167	167	William Adamson..........	146	146
(Esta.) De Jongh	77	77	Jas. Cunningham..........	21	21
Roger Pinckney...........	49	49	John Chestnut Est.........	2	2
Wm. S. Price.............	21	21	R. L. Champion Est........	2	3
Mary McLeod.............	26	26	Zach Canty Est............	182	183
Joseph E. Jenkins.........	24	24	Sarah Canty..............	23	23
Esta. Jeremiah Miles.......	109	110	H. H. Dickinson Est.......	13	13
Esta. John Boyle..........	57	59	Harriet English...........	87	87
John V. Ashe	114	114	John Robertson............	41	41
Benj'n Whaley............	52	52	John Taylor..............	134	134
Esta. Benj'n Bailey........	38	38			
Eliza Swinton.............	34	34	*Laurens County*		
Susan E. Smith...........	36	36	H. Norton...............	9	9
St. George's Parish			LEXINGTON COUNTY		
Thomas Gates.............	101	101	William Geiger............	2	2
Elizabeth Poyas...........	36	36	Jacob Barrett.............	45	45
Morton A. Waring.........	21	21	H. B. Brickell............	4	4
Mary S. Legare...........	42	42	Estate of J. D. Reese.......	20	20
William L. Smith..........	39	39	Wm. Clarkson.............	137	137
F. Vanderlippe............	7	7	Estate of Joel Adams Senr...	104	104
(Esta.) F. Perry	30	30	Estate of Jno. Howell.......	74	74
John Johnson Jun;.........	20	20	Jos. A. Brevard...........	17	17
			Estate of Wm. Leadingham..	27	27
St. John's Colleton			Estate of James Pearse......	31	33
Christopher Jenkins........	97	97	Estate of H. W. Adams.....	58	59
Andrew Milne.............	120	120	Estate of Scott's...........	124	125
James Legare..............	49	49	S. Green's Plantation.......	51	51
Thomas Legare............	81	81			
Est. Thomas Mathews......	80	80	*Columbia*		
B. D. Roper..............	71	71	F. H. Elmore.............	3	3
Susannah Whitter..........	42	44	J. & W. McMillon.........	17	17
Est. M. Jenkens...........	66	66			
Est. Jenkens..............	125	125	*Marion County*		
Est. Sheerman............	21	21	Alston Robert............	5	5
E. M. Seabrook...........	52	52			
Est. R. Waistcoat..........	16	16	MARLBORO COUNTY		
T. B. Seabrook...........	52	52	John Dewet..............	53	53
Trust Est. E. Bailey........	28	28	Josiah J. Evans...........	80	80
Est. Ashe................	61	61	John O'neal for Alexr. Mc-		
James C. Meggett..........	27	27	Iver...................	46	46
Mrs. E. La Roche..........	43	43	Alexander Sparks.........	76	76
			Dixon Hestle for H. Marshall	31	31
Edgefield County			Alexander McIntosh........	34	34
R. McDonald..............	3	3	Patty Jackson............	2	2
Nancy Coleman...........	11	11	Caleb Isgate for C. Mande-		
			ville..................	54	54
Fairfield County			Francis McBryde..........	3	3
James B. Pickett..........	15	15			
Robert Adams.............	40	40	ORANGEBURGH COUNTY		
John Thomas.............	58	58	*St. Matthew's Parish*		
Esta. of Woodward by W.			Adam Keitt Est............	33	33
Strother...............	19	19	John McCord Est.........	95	95
			John Murph Slaves in St.		
Greenville County			Matthew's Parish........	42	42
Thomas McCarroll.........	16	16			

SOUTH CAROLINA—*Continued*

Name	Slaves	Total	Name	Slaves	Total
St. Matthews Parish—Cont.			Plantation of Stephen O.		
Richard Singleton Slaves in			Miller.................	87	88
St. Matthew's Parish True-			Plantation Joseph Berod....	4	4
blew Plantation..........	204	204	Plantation of James S. Deas.	155	155
Mary A. Thompson Est.....	49	49	Estate R. L. Champion.....	188	188
Paul Warley Jr. Slaves Rich-			Estate John P. Richardson ..	70	71
mond St. Matthew's Parish.	67	67	Estate John G. Davis.......	110	114
Catherine Raoul Slaves in St.			Estate Gabriel W. Dingle....	20	24
Matthew's Parish Bell-			Plantation James B. Richard-		
ville...................	90	92	son Jr...................	59	60
			Plantation John McCanr....	18	19
SPARTANBURG COUNTY			Plantation Samuel Boykin...	39	40
Rose Benson.............	1	1	Plantation James Taylor....	35	35
			Est. of Mathew S. Moore Jr..	60	62
Sumter County			Plantation of William Wattes	20	20
Estate John McFaddin......	38	38	Estate of John Singleton....	310	315
Estate of Thomas McFaddin.	18	18	Estate of William R. Theus..	50	59
Estate of Eli McFaddin.....	73	73			
Estate Phillip Carolan	18	18	UNION COUNTY		
Plantation of Samuel and			Mrs. Angelica Nott........	58	58
Samuel A. Mavinch	31	31	Richard Pickering for Col.		
Estate of Matthew S. Moore			Myers.................	121	122
Sr.....................	42	42	William Norris............	3	3
Plantation R. Hunt........	9	9	Solomon Moore (overseer)...	43	44
Fedrick Miers Plantation....	18	18			
Plantation of G. W. Barnes..	4	4	WILLIAMSBURGH COUNTY		
Estate M. A. Murrel (?).....	27	27	Francis Cordes............	87	87
Estate Huldy Nettles.......	20	20	Wm. Dollard Est..........	22	22
Plantation of Charles D.			Eliza Dollard.............	9	9
Brown................	82	82	Martha Gibson............	2	2
Plantation of Frank Cord...	72	72	Alexander Glass...........	18	18
Estate John Tindale........	12	12	Robt. McCutchen..........	28	28
Plantation of Thomas C.			Est. Samuel Miller.........	5	5
Richardson.............	30	30	Est. Wm. Murrell.........	8	8
Plantation of John Canty....	20	20	Est. Samuel Nesmith.......	10	10
Estate of Epps............	15	16	William Tistall............	17	17
Estate of Samuel Witherspoon	52	53	Est. R. L. Witherspoon.....	54	54

TENNESSEE

Name	Slaves	Total	Name	Slaves	Total
BEDFORD COUNTY			William Hayden...........	3	3
Martha Goodwin..........	12	13	Est. of James Thomas......	1	1
			Est. of Catharine Knox......	4	4
CARROLL COUNTY			Heirs of Wm. Kemp........	1	1
Henry Forest.............	5	5	Est. of Joel Lewis..........	1	1
			Charles J. Love............	3	3
DAVIDSON COUNTY			John McNairy.............	4	4
Joseph Ewing.............	7	7	Est. of Edward Potts.......	4	4
Boyd McNairy............	11	11	Isaac Sitler...............	1	1
Jas. Overton.............	23	23	Est. of Michael Stean.......	2	2
Alexr. Porter.............	29	29	George Wilson.............	1	1
Andrew Morrison..........	5	5			
			DICKSON COUNTY		
Town of Nashville			Montgomery Bell..........	7	7
Est. of F. Crockett........	1	1			
Est. of James Edwards......	4	4	FRANKLIN COUNTY		
Heirs of Lewis Faulkner	1	1	Dyer Moore's list of Negroes		
Est. of Absalum Hooper.....	2	2	in this County..........	9	9

TENNESSEE—*Continued*

Name	Slaves	Tota.	Name	Slaves	Total
GILES COUNTY			SHELBY COUNTY		
Willis Potress..............	11	11	P. Mahar Heirs............	2	2
			Charles..................	1	1
HAYWOOD COUNTY			Isaac....................	7	7
Saml. Jordan..............	10	10	A. H. Morelle.............	3	3
			Heirs of D. Finney........	4	4
HUMPHREYS COUNTY					
Daniel Mason.............	37	37	STEWART COUNTY		
			Sally Williams............	28	29
KNOX COUNTY					
Knoxville			SULLIVAN COUNTY		
Belinda Grainger...........	1	1	James King...............	16	16
Thomas Crutchfield........	5	5	Richard Chester...........	1	1
LINCOLN COUNTY			TIPTON COUNTY		
Peter Bright..............	6	6	Jacob Miswanger..........	13	13
Carolina Burford..........	6	6	William B. Pryor..........	5	5
David Burford.............	4	4			
			WASHINGTON COUNTY		
MAURY COUNTY			Polly Love's estate........	8	10
Will Polk.................	96	97			
Gerrard T. Greenfield......	46	46	WILLIAMSON COUNTY		
P. B. Degraftenreid........	59	59	Henry Halfacre............	15	15
			Hezekiah Puryear..........	34	34
MONTGOMERY COUNTY			William H. Hilliard........	6	6
Joshua Elder..............	6	6	Martin Adams.............	1	1
William Garrett...........	5	5	Estate of J. Branch........	2	2
			J. D. Bennett for S. Parrish..	8	8
			Penelope Edney...........	5	5
RHEA COUNTY			Abraham Dunway..........	23	23
William Walker............	5	5	William McCutchan.......	5	5
			Ransom Cates.............	5	5
ROBERTSON COUNTY			Thomas Stacy.............	50	50
Inage Whites Quarter.......	4	4	Loderick Beach............	4	4
Robert Wimberley..........	1	1	Lewis W. Reves............	1	1
Vincent Williams...........	5	5	William Johnson...........	2	2
Jessee Williams.............	15	15	Thomas Money............	13	13
			William B. McClellan.......	4	4
			William G. Children........	6	6
RUTHERFORD COUNTY			William Maney............	46	46
V. D. Cowen..............	14	14	Robert P. Curren..........	10	10
Moses R. Buckhanon.......	1	1	William Read.............	3	3
Levi Alexander............	6	6			

VIRGINIA

Name	Slaves	Total	Name	Slaves	Total
ACCOMACK COUNTY			Stephen Pitts..............	2	2
Saint George's Parish			Wm. H. West (Slaves on		
Peter Kellam..............	4	4	Farm).................	7	7
Sally Leatherberry.........	2	2			
Mathew Townsend........	4	4	ALBEMARLE COUNTY		
Michel P. Underhill........	6	6	David Anderson (by Agt.)...	15	15
			Colby Cowards (Estate).....	26	26
			William Dickinsons (estate)..	2	2
Accomack Parish			Thomas & Hopkins (Estate).	2	2
Leah Bloxom..............	2	2	Joseph Hawkins...........	3	3
George Bayne.............	4	4	Nancy Page's (Estate)......	4	4
Wm. Dickinson...........	3	3	James Lyndsays (Estate)....	31	31
Stephen Hickman..........	5	5	Charles Parrotts (Estate)....	7	7
Maria Parramore..........	4	4	Henry Rives (Estate).......	16	16
Leah Parramore...........	5	5			

VIRGINIA—*Continued*

Name	Slaves	Total	Name	Slaves	Total
ALBEMARLE COUNTY—*Cont.*			Pricella Watts............	5	5
Robert Rives (by Agent)....	39	39	Fortune Dunn.............	2	2
Charles A. Scotts (Estate)....	22	22	Dinah Spriggs.............	2	2
Thomas Hopkins (Estate)...	2	2	Nancy Shepherd...........	2	2
John Walters (Estate)......	3	3	Aunt Grace...............	2	2
			Peggy Jennings...........	5	5
Norfolk Parish			Venus Ruffin.............	5	5
Frank Hatton.............	4	4	Julia Magagnas...........	3	3
Mary Happer.............	4	4	Aunt Violet..............	2	2
John Thompson...........	3	3	Toney Hopkins...........	2	2
			Charles Nickolson.........	3	3
Elizabeth River Parish					
Samuel Holt..............	1	1	*Briggs Point*		
Samuel Johnson..........	2	2	Rose McCane.............	4	4
Raymond Jarvis...........	3	3	Margeret White..........	2	2
Portsmouth Parish			*Bermuda Street*		
Holt Wilson..............	13	13	Bill Fortune..............	3	3
Benjamin Alford..........	7	7	Pricilla Shepherd..........	1	1
Richard Blow.............	11	11	Kitty Bissell..............	3	3
			Nic Johnson..............	5	5
E. R. P.			L. Claiborne..............	4	4
Horatio Moore............	1	1			
Joel Callis...............	7	7	*Union Street and Vicinity*		
			Peggy Selden.............	2	2
			Peggy Berry..............	6	6
St. Brides Parish					
Caleb Wilson.............	17	17	*Cumberland Street*		
Samuel Bartee............	19	19	James Baker.............	8	8
Nathaniel Wilson, Jr.......	10	10	Peggy Starke............	7	7
Robert B. Butt...........	32	32	Fanny Thorogood.........	3	3
George Newton...........	19	19	Patsey Phillips...........	4	4
			Letty Byrd...............	3	3
St. B. P.			Martha Eilbeck...........	2	2
Jacob Keeling............	5	5	Racheal Prescott..........	3	3
William Portlock..........	2	2	Rose Hansford........	8	8
Norfolk Boro			*Catherine Street & Vicinity*		
Princess Anne Road			Nelly Robertson...........	6 (?)	6
Elisha C. White...........	7	7	Racheal Armistead.........	2 (?)	2
Daniel Ash...............	4	4	Jack Whitfield............	7 (?)	11
John Jacobs..............	2	2	Betsey Clarke............	1	1
			Old Sarah Camp..........	7	7
Church Street			Gabriel Robertson.........	5	5
America Dawley..........	2	2	Phillip Gorden............	2	2
Dr. T. Lawson............	2	2	Judy Boush..............	11	11
John White..............	5	5	Jack Johnson.............	3	3
Peter Roberts............	2	2	Mary James..............	3	3
Sam Lawey...............	2	2			
Dick White..............	4	4	*Brewer Street*		
Phillip Lee..............	6	6	Peggy Walker............	3	3
George Carey.............	3	3			
Gabriel Talbot...........	8	8	*Granby Street*		
Maria Thorogood.........	5 (?)	5	Mary Baush..............	7	7
Phillis Nimmo...........	1	1	Rose Bright..............	3	3
Judy Carter..............	1	1			
Solomon Wilson..........	2	2	*Queen Street*		
Ellen Emmerson..........	2	2	Nancy Green.............	1	1

VIRGINIA—*Continued*

Name	Slaves	Total	Name	Slaves	Total
Queen Street—Cont.			Bernard Booker............	16	16
Elisha Cotton..............	4	4	Est. Jno. M. Walker........	18	18
Kitty Waddey.............	3	3	Alexander Mundy..........	11	11
Tamer Currier.............	4	4			
			AUGUSTA COUNTY		
Smith Point			Chapman Johnson.........	33	33
Miss Armstead............	4	4	David W. Patterson........	4	4
			John Watson..............	5	5
Free Mason Street			William Young............	7	7
Mary Watts...............	4	4			
Rose Dunn................	4	4	BEDFORD COUNTY		
			Cabell & Leftwich..........	23	23
Little Water Street			Mary Hurt................	18	18
Peggy Wilson..............	2	2	Burr Garland.............	9	9
Frank Mercer.............	3	3			
Stephen Jasper............	2	2	BRUNSWICK COUNTY		
			James Lewis (?) Junr.......	11	11
Woodsides Lane and Wharf			David Meridith est........	19	20
Lydia Keeling.............	3	3			
			BUCKINGHAM COUNTY		
Commerce Street			Peter Stratton Jr..........	5	5
John Tunis...............	7	7	Edward Booker............	3	3
			Rivers & White............	13	13
Main Street			John C. Page..............	33	33
Miss Watson..............	2	2	Seymour Holman..........	3	3
Harrison Almond..........	3	3	Dillis' Company...........	4	4
Miss P. Proby.............	5	5	Est. Joseph Eades..........	14	14
T. Nixon.................	2	2	Est. Jas. Staton...........	8	8
			Molley Hughes (?).........	5	5
AMELIA COUNTY			Est. Thos. Wingfield.......	7	7
Catherine P. H. Jones......	22	22	John Dunlap..............	6	6
Est. George Jones..........	40	40			
George L. Scott..........	9	9	CABELL COUNTY		
Frances B. Epes...........	21	21	John Allison..............	4	4
Est. Frances Jones.........	27	27			
Samuel Scott.............	24	24	CAMPBELL COUNTY		
Est. Christian Gilliam......	50	50	Colin Buckner............	57	57
Anderson F. Clay..........	3	3	Mary Brown..............	5	5
John C. Hill..............	7	7	William Daniel (Judge).....	14	14
Est. John S. Hardaway.....	24	24	Augustine Leftwich........	36	36
Ben. S. Meade.............	2	2	George K. Lamberth.......	5	5
			William McKinney........	36	36
AMHERST COUNTY			David G. Murrell..........	4	4
Est. Ambrose Tomlinson....	9	9	James B. Risque...........	5	5
Est. Preston H. Garland....	9	9	Wiatt Pettyjohn...........	7	7
Seth Woodroof............	7	7	John M. Warwick..........	4	4
Philip St. George Ambler....	47	47			
William Morgan...........	67	67	*Lynchburg*		
Francis Coleman...........	14	14	William J. Isbill...........	3	3
Shelton Wright............	6	6			
Archibald Robertson.......	51	51	CAROLINE COUNTY		
Claibourne W. Gooch.......	13	13	Ann Baylor...............	30	30
Timothy Fletcher..........	4	4	George W. Gatewood.......	8	8
Jno. Wilson..............	12	12	John Martin..............	1	1
Nathaniel Floyd (?)........	4 (?)	4	William Puller............	16	16
William Owens............	5	5	Edwin Upshaw............	8	8
Henry Langhorne..........	3	3			
Mary Brown..............	12	12			

VIRGINIA—*Continued*

Name	Slaves	Tota.	Name	Slaves	Total
Charles City County			John F. May.............	9	9
John P. Burton............	23	23	Edward Watkins..........	62	62
Susan Oglesby.............	7	7			
John Colgin...............	11	11	*Petersburg*		
			Thos. Jones..............	2	2
Charlotte County			Upper Appomattox C......	5	5
Est. Archer Hatchett.......	24	24	Richard Sturdivant........	8	8
James Bruce (L. P. C.)......	88	88	Patsey Green.............	2	2
Est. William Barksdale......	9	9	Eliza Pegram's Estate.......	7	8
			Daniel Starke.............	2	2
Chesterfield County			William E. Borsseau........	2	2
Ruben Raglin.............	6	6	Mary Harrison.............	2	2
Bevely Randolph..........	9	9	Edward Archer............	5	5
Thomas P. Hare...........	5	5	Wilson C. Stith...........	1	1
William Corling............	10	10	Henry Harrison...........	3	3
Eady Jackson.............	4	4	James Dunlop.............	3	3
Richard C. Gillum.........	2	2	James Prentis.............	2	2
Estate James Bray.........	24	24	Street Commissioners.......	3	5
John Clarke...............	25	25			
Javes Watkins.............	2	2	**Elizabeth City County**		
Robert B. Wells...........	13	13	*Old Point*		
Elizabeth Voden...........	5	5	John Ruffin..............	1	1
			Caty Thomas.............	4	4
Culpeper County			Rose Russell..............	3	3
Jas. Payne, Quarter........	7	7	Lucy Stepney.............	3	3
John P. Kelly's (quarter at			Mariah Hamm (?).........	3	3
mill)...................	35	41			
William Morton's (Estate)...	25	25	**Essex County**		
William Mitchell Jr. (Estate).	6	6	Livingston Murcoe's Estate..	1	2
William Smith (Estate Madi-			John S. Spindle............	16	16
son Line)...............	9	9			
Rd. Norris (Estate).........	54	54	**Fairfax County**		
Geo. Buckner's (Estate).....	20	21	Lucinda Carter............	5	5
Newmans Allen's (Estate)...	15	15	Thomas Ingraham.........	2	2
Thos. Shirley's (Estate).....	13	13	Bernard Hooe.............	4	4
Henry Barnes (Est.)........	13	17	Thomas Triplett...........	13	13
J. Harris (Estate)..........	8	8	Robert Hunter............	25	25
Jerry Pannel (Estate).......	12	12	William Bruen............	5	5
G. Walls (Estate)..........	8	8	Alexander Moore...........	1	1
Wm. Gibson's (Estate)......	19	19	James McDaniel...........	14	14
Wm. Nerron's (estate)......	6	6	Nehemiah Davis...........	7	7
Wm. Cook's (estate)........	7	7			
			Fauquier County		
Cumberland County			J. Gill, Overseer for Foote...	6	6
Wm. Frayser, Jr. agent (the			Bednigo (Foreman French's		
same) for Martha B. Eppes	24	24	Quarter)................	17	17
Benj. Hobson..............	12	12	Jas. Carr (overseer for Hor-		
Benj. Hatcher.............	45	45	ner)...................	25	29
Wm. McLaurine...........	5	5	William Shenher's Quarter..	21	21
Est. Judy Randolph........	18	21	Lewis Lumpkin (Overseer		
			Martin)................	21	21
Dinwiddie County			John Waldens (quarter).....	11	11
William B. Hamblin........	18	18	J. Marshalls (Quarter)......	22	22
Daniel Southall...........	2	2	Thomas Hillery (overseer for		
Eliza Goodwyn............	40	40	Marshall)...............	21	21
William Haxall............	12	12	Mrs. Thompson, Negroes in		
John Grammar............	15	15	Warrenton..............	6	6
Michael Roper............	2	2			

VIRGINIA—*Continued*

Name	Slaves	Total	Name	Slaves	Total
FAQUIER COUNTY—*Cont.*			GREENBRIAR COUNTY		
Joseph Hudnell (overseer for Shenher)	11	12	Andrew Alexander	2	2
Aaron Bise (Quarter)	2	2	GREENSVILLE COUNTY		
G. B. Hitch (overseer for Dixon's estate);	125	125	Benjamin Williamson's Quarter	4	4
Dr. T. T. Withers (quarter)	27	27	Richard B. Grigg's Quarter	8	16
William Anderson	2	2	David B. Mason's quarter	34	39
William Waters (farm)	6	6	Negro Esther Without owner or home	1	1
Mrs. Wallace (farm)	3	3			
William Homers (Farm)	18	18	Negroes Ben & Tener without owner	2	2
Nathaniel Mocrae U. S. A.	6	6	James Blank's Estate	16	20
Catharine Ramsey	6	6	John Ivey's Quarter	4	4
			John A. Person's Quarter	3	4
FLUVANNA COUNTY			Green Turner's Estate	8	8
Strange & Jones	2	2			
Franklin Trice's Quarter	17	17	HALIFAX COUNTY		
Wm. A. Baker (of Hanover)	5	5	Thomas Anderson	3	3
John Carter of Henrico & John Carter, his son	1	1	Isaac Coles Est	61	61
			William Dews	5	5
FRANKLIN COUNTY			Mack Delany	3	3
William A. Burwell Est	101	101	William Elam	14	14
Jessee Hackwood Est	8	8	Robert Easley	8	8
Booker Preston	22	22	Joseph Friend	11	11
			Robert Harriston	15	15
FREDERICK COUNTY			Edmund Irby's Est	40	40
Eastern District			Thomas Munford	5	5
George Hall	2	2	William Moseley	13	13
Thomas F. Nelson	23	23	Samuel Pannell	47	47
John E. Page Exr	31	31	Samuel Ragland Est	4	4
John Webb	5	5	John Randolph	24	24
			Henry Theriatt	16	16
Western District			James W. Thomas	12	12
Joseph Pennybaker	1	1	Paul Venable	23	23
Elizabeth Green	6	6	James Vaughan	14	14
John Jordan	1	1	William M. Watkins	23	23
George W. Keger	1	1	Abram W. Wimbish	34	34
Clarissa Larve	1	1	Rawley White	5	5
			Stephen Worsham	2	2
GLOUCESTER COUNTY			Susan Younger's Est	2	2
Thomas R. Corr	6	6	Rodger Adkisson's Est	13	13
Thomas Roane	1	1	William Baird	18	18
			Elizabeth Bull	5	5
GOOCHLAND COUNTY			Alexr. Cunningham	34	34
Robert R. Watkins	6	6	Clemt. Carrington	62	62
Zackariah McGinder	3	3	Humbreston Skipwith	87	87
Hezekiah Henley	2	2			
Joseph Woodson	2	2	HAMPSHIRE COUNTY		
Jack Cox	4	4	Nancy Armstrong	2	2
William Mountjory	9	9	Samuel Kercheval	3	3
William Shelton	1	1	Agnes Morrison	5	5
Wesley Wright	3	3	Simon Taylor	10	10
Thomas Drumwright (?)	2	2	John Wright	9	9
Thomas Bolling	30	30			
Overton B. Pettitt	42	42	HANOVER COUNTY		
Margaret Richardson	6	6	James Lyons	17	17
William Crawford	7	7			

VIRGINIA—*Continued*

Name	Slaves	Total	Name	Slaves	Total
HANOVER COUNTY—*Cont.*			Mann Satterwhite..........	2	2
Garland Thompson (Rich-			John H. Ustace.............	2	2
mond).................	2	2	Josiah B. Abbott...........	2	2
Lucy Berkeley.............	3	3	Jesse H. Turner............	3	3
William S. Wights (est.)	4	4	Edwin Porter..............	6	6
Sarah H. Vest.............	5	5	David Barclay.............	3	3
Spotswood Mosby (Rich.) ...	1	1	William Moncure..........	2	2
			William Goodnow..........	4	4
HENRICO COUNTY			David Barclay.............	3	3
Cambridge a Slave, the prop-			Sarah Brooke (William		
erty of Jesse Williams—2..	2	2	Young, agent)...........	4	4
Elizabeth Blaky (of Rich-					
mond).................	6	6	*City of Richmond*		
Cole Muse................	3	3	*Monroe Ward*		
Archibald Blair (Richmond)	2	2	Dr. Charles Abrams........	1	1
Richard C. Wortham (Rich-			Benjamin Ames............	4	4
mond).................	1	1	Henry Anderson...........	2	2
Adam Craig's Estate......	7	7	Richard Anderson..........	3	3
Benjamin Mann...........	3	3	David J. Burr & Co........	8	8
Doct. Taylor (Chesterfield)..	1	1	Nathaniel Bailey..........	1	1
Richard Denny............	1	1	Mary Blair................	5	5
Byrd George..............	24	24	Mr. Broadus...............	1	1
Rich^d. Young for Miss Wil-			John Bosher...............	4	4
liamson................	2	2	Dr. Bohannan.............	1	1
Selina Brooke (Richmond)...	4	4	John Burton...............	1	1
James Bosher (of Richmond)	5	5	David Barclay.............	1	1
Benjamin Mosly's est.......	2	4	Campbell Blades...........	1	1
John Goddin..............	8	8	George M. Branch.........	1	1
Frederick Jude............	4	4	Thos. B. Bigger............	1	1
William D. Wrenn..........	6	6	I. J. Cohen................	4	4
William Price.............	17	17	Dr. Clark.................	6	6
John Burton's Estate.......	2	2	Cunningham & Anderson....	2	2
French & Jordan...........	12	12	Samuel Dunn..............	9	9
Archibald Blair (Richmond).	9	9	Margaret Digges..........	4	4
Thomas Ritchie (of Do.)	5	5	Davenport's Estate........	3	3
Norman Norton...........	7	7	Mrs. Dugar...............	1	1
Richard Edwards (of Rich-			Samuel Coe...............	1	1
mond).................	3	3	John Enders..............	1	1
Godfrey Walder (of Do.)	2	2	George D. Fisher..........	1	1
John Mosley..............	9	9	Francis Foster............	1	1
Judith Nelson.............	3	3	Mrs. Fleisher's estate	5	5
Edmund B. Granger........	5	5	Tom Fox..................	1	1
Bowler Cocke's Estate......	5	6	John Fisher...............	1	1
John Fraser..............	2	2	Temple Qwathmey.........	5	5
William B. Jennings Mgr. for			Goode's estate	2	2
Geo. Cox...............	43	44	Susan Hatcher............	4	4
Mary Sharp (of Norfolk)....	5	5	Thomas Hooper...........	2	2
William G. Keesee.........	7	7	Daniel Hatcher............	4	4
Nelson Cary..............	20	20	John Heron...............	3	3
Harriett Thompson........	2	2	Margaret Hylton..........	4	4
Smith & Gordon's Coal pitts.	35	35	M. W. Hancock...........	1	1
Johnson Eubank...........	3	3	Jinny Hill................	1	1
Maurice Primrose..........	7	7	Walter Jones..............	1	1
George M. Carrington......	4	4	Taylor Jackson............	2	2
William F. Micse..........	2	2	William Johnson...........	4	4
Andrew Sweeny...........	7	7	Richard Loving............	1	1
John Robinson............	5	5	Joseph Leake..............	6	6
Peter V. Daniel...........	5	5	Dr. Benjn. Lewis..........	1	1

VIRGINIA—*Continued*

Name	Slaves	Total	Name	Slaves	Total
City of Richmond Monroe Ward—Cont.			J. J. Cohen	1	1
			John G. Crouch	4	4
Benjamin Mosby's estate	3	3	Carey, Nelson & Co	5	5
Joe Morris	1	1	Davenport & Allen	2	2
Miller & Sampson	10	10	Mrs. Dudley	1	1
Samuel S. Myers & Co	82	82	William Finney	1	1
Logan McCoul	1	1	James Gentry	3	3
Charles McMurdo	1	1	Wm. & Wm. Galt, Jr.	1	1
Thomas Owen	1	1	Gray & Pankey	1	1
Fisher & Price	6	6	Robert R. Glenn	3	3
William Poe	1	1	Richd. C. Gilliam	55	55
Lucy Price	3	3	Anthony J. Gouvea	14	14
Ferral Price	1	1	Jack Harris	1	1
Thomas Priddy	1	1	James Harrison	2	2
Charles Poke	2	2	Holt & Ross	1	1
Reeves Price	4	4	P. Houston	1	1
George Picket	2	2	Hutchison & Kerr	36	36
David Ross	1	1	Carey Harris	2	2
Wm. H. Richardson	4	4	A. Hughes	1	1
Peyton Randolph's estate	2	2	Mary Hart	1	1
Sally Smith	3	3	Thomas T. Johnson	1	1
John Shepard	2	2	Susan Kimbrough	3	3
Mr. Sutton	1	1	Alfred King	1	1
Charles Smith	1	1	Lewis's estate	1	1
A. Saunders	2	2	James McDildoe	3	3
Edmund Tompkins	7	7	Garland H. Mitchell	1	1
Jaquelin Taylor	1	1	Samuel Murray	1	1
Christian Turner	5	5	John McCage	3	3
Frederick Woodson	2	2	Wilson Morris	1	1
William Wickham	1	1	Reuben Moss	1	1
Mosby Woodson	2	2	Mosby & Young	24	25
Lewis Wingfield	1	1	George Mastin	1	1
Mrs. Winfree	3	3	Catharine McCall's estate	4	4
Thomas Woodson	1	1	William Nekervis	1	1
Richard C. Wortham	1	1	Otis, Dunlop & Co	8	8
Letty Wingfield	5	5	William F. Pendleton	4	4
Joseph Watkins	1	1	A. Petticolas & Co	1	1
James Yarrington	1	1	Samuel Putney	5	5
			Beverly Randolph	3	3
Madison Ward			Wilton Randolph's estate	2	2
Thomas Atkinson	1	1	Ralston & Pleasants	1	1
John Allen, jr.	15	15	Thomas Rutherford	1	1
Doctor Archer	3	3	William J. Robertson	3	3
Richd. Anderson & Co	53	53	James Scott	1	1
Richd. Anderson	1	1	Thomas Smith	5	5
John Allan	1	1	Andrew Sweeny	4	4
John Armistead	1	1	Joseph Selden	6	6
Col. Lawson Burfoot	8	8	Beverly Skipwith	3	3
Gurdon H. Bacchus	1	1	George E. Tiffin	1	1
Binford, Brooks & Co	1	1	Jefferson E. Trice	1	1
John Binford	1	1	Philip M. Tabb	5	5
William Barret	15	15	Archibald Thomas	3	3
Nath. Bowe's (decd.) estate	4	4	Susan Turner	1	1
John Barr	3	3	Patsy Underwood	1	1
James Brandon	4	4	Daniel Warwick	1	1
Dr. James Blair	4	4	William Wickham (Hanover)	2	2
Leonard Cooly	7	7	James H. Walthall	46	46
George P. Crump	3	3	William Young	1	1

VIRGINIA—*Continued*

Name	Slaves	Total	Name	Slaves	Total
Jefferson Ward			Martimer Roper	3	3
Mark Anthony	1	1	Lewis Rogers	2	2
Thomas Adkins	71	71	James Ratliffe	1	1
John Anderson	1	1	Benjm. Stetson	3	3
Robert Anderson	1	1	James Scott	1	1
Catherine E. Adams	4	4	Andrew Smith	3	3
Carter Braxton's estate	4	4	Smith & Johnson	1	1
William R. Butler	10	10	Patrick Slaughter	1	1
Baldwin, Ives & Co	1	1	Thomas Smith	2	2
Joseph Bohannan	2	2	Charlotte Saunders	2	2
John W. Beers	5	5	Geo. Semple's estate	2	2
Moses Branch	2	2	William Shepperson	4	4
Thomas Berry	1	1	Martha Sansum	1	1
John Burton	4	4	Thomas Turner	1	1
Dr. James Blair	1	1	Ira Tickenor	5	5
William & Thomas Burton	8	9	John Van-Lew & Co	1	1
Elizabeth Blackwood	4	4	Thomas West	5	5
David Barclay	74	74	Keziah Wilkerson	2	2
Geo. Booker, Agt. of Dock			Alfred Wherry	40	40
Company	2	2	Whitlock & Wicker	2	3
Stephen Cowley	7	7	Robert Williamson	3	3
J. Crane	1	1	William Wickham	5	5
Revd. Mr. Charlton	2	2	Henry Wade	1	1
Henry L. Carter	3	3	William Wren, g'rdn. of Jas.		
John Clarke	3	3	Price	5	5
John L. Carter	2	2	Charles Wills	3	3
John Clarke, (Charles City)	3	3			
Philip Claiborne	1	1	HENRY COUNTY		
Thomas Davidson	2	2	Harden Hairston (non-res.)	7	7
Robert Davis	3	3	John A. Hairston (non-res.)	7	7
John Epperson	1	1	Samuel Hairston (non-res.)	50	50
Mourning Foster	5	5	Lucinda Redd (non-res.)	52	52
Simon Frayser	1	1			
Franklin & Hardgrove	32	32	ISLE OF WIGHT COUNTY		
Edward Farrar	2	2	Albert Moody Inft	1	1
Benjm. Green	3	3	Robert Lawrence of Nod (?)	3	3
S. C. Golden	2	2	Penelope Pitt	6	6
Joshua Goode	16	16	Sally Powell of Nansd	2	2
William Goodnow	1	1	John Urquhart, sr	2	2
Mr. Hayes	5	5	Silas Summerel So. (?)	6	6
E. & A. Hubbard	1	1	Christopher Reynolds Nd	2	2
Nancy Horn	1	1	Copha Wilkins Est	1	1
John King	4	4	William Goodwin Est	3	3
Thomas Lewis	2	2	Andrew Woodleys Est	20	20
James Ligons	1	1	Matt. Wills Est	1	1
William Meriam	1	1	Richard H. Cocke (Surry)	2	2
Joseph H. Mayo	1	1	William D. Henly	2	2
Mordecai Marx	1	1	George J. Byrd of No.	3	3
Benjm. Mosby's estate	4	4	Nancy Vellines	1	1
John Otway Mosby	1	1	William White's Est	2	2
John Marshall	1	1	Louisa Pierce of Surry	9	9
John Myers	4	4	John Riley of Nor.	4	4
Sarah Montague	2	2	Thomas & Stringfield	2	2
Frances Nelson	1	1	John B. Levy of Nor.	5	5
William Palmer	4	4			
Thomas Pulling	1	1	JAMES CITY COUNTY		
Thomas Priddy	2	2	Newsum & Layalls Est	5	5
Fleming Roper	2	2	Thomas Coleman	33	33

VIRGINIA—*Continued*

Name	Slaves	Total	Name	Slaves	Total
JAMES CITY COUNTY—*Cont.*			Estate of James Corben	35	35
Thomas G. Peachy	4	4	KING WILLIAM COUNTY		
Mary Ann Peachy	13	13	John C. Tunstall's (slaves)	8	8
Jane Cary's Est	4	4	Stirling Lipscomb (overseer)	34	42
Thomas Lands	7	7	Alexander King's (slaves)	7	7
Geo. W. P. Custer by Wm. Bromley his Stewd	101	110	Joseph H. Travis' (slaves)		
			Charles Johnson and overseer	29	33
JEFFERSON COUNTY			Sarah R. Richardson and overseer	13	21
John Briscoe	7	7	George W. P. Custis by Thomas B. Martin	54	55
William Brown	9	9	William P. Taylor by Peter Campbell	52	57
Henry Hanes	4	4	Judith B. Hill and overseer	25	29
Jacob Hanes	6	6	Catherine Richerson and overseer	1	10
Mary Manning	24	24	Thomas Hill and overseer	14	18
Elizabeth Pendleton	1	1	Christopher Johnson and overseers	96	109
James L. Ransom	5	5	Isaac Quarles and overseer	16	31
William Robinson	7	7	Robert Hill by Nath'l Aeree	15	17
Susan B. Taylor	28	28	Thomas Carter and overseer	114	120
Alexander War	6	6	John W. Tomlin by Littleberry Taylor	47	48
KING AND QUEEN COUNTY			Jacquelin A. Berkley by Temple Moore	32	33
Ro: B. Semple	31	31	Lewis Berkley by Chas. Dodson	57	62
William Pollard	7	7	John W. Homes by Richard S. Pruett	31	33
Henry Lumpkin, Jr	2	2	Thomas C. Nelson and overseer	96	106
Dianna Lumpkin	11	11	George N. Powill and overseer	16	25
Carter B. Fogg	14	14	Ann E. Vass and overseer	29	33
Mary Haws	18	18	Mary Munday and overseer	42	45
Mary Garnett	2	2	Charles L. Hincher and overseer	15	18
Philip Brooks (overseer for John Jones)	6	6	Geo. W. Bassett by John W. Street	47	52
Tho. L. Fauntleroy	19	19	Philip Sylett and overseer	78	86
Peter Clayton (overseer for Tho. Walker)	8	8	LANCASTER COUNTY		
John W. Watkins (overseer for J. Garnett's sepr. (?))	12	12	Baldwin Smith	1	1
Kauffman Gresham	1	1	LOUDOUN COUNTY *Leesburg*		
Holland Godwins Gdm. who is Richard Godwin	3	3	David Carr's Slaves	2	2
Harriot Brumley	4	4	James Harris	2	2
Tho. Edwards (overseer for Jacob D. Walkers sepr. (?))	19	19	On Josiah Murray's plantation	3	3
Tho. Jones	12	12	LOUISA COUNTY		
John Richards, Senr	4	4	Joseph Shelton of Goochland	31	31
Monitre D. Spencer Adm. D. Diggs	4	4	John Waldrope (Henrico)?	6	6
Ro. B. Boyds Gdm	23	23	LUNENBURG COUNTY		
Tho. Edwards (overseer for Peter T. Pollard)	14	14	Richard Puryear	5	5
Henry Fleming (overseer for Tho. Smith ex or (?))	72	72			
James C. Roy	15	15			
Jas. R. Irson (overseer for Thomas Collins)	11	12			
KING GEORGE COUNTY					
Est. Geo: Turner, Decd	38	38			
Est. Wm. Bernard, Jr. Decd	37	37			
John C. Brown's Estate	4	4			

VIRGINIA—*Continued*

Name	Slaves	Total
MADISON COUNTY		
John Kobler	7	7
(?) John Maggert	2	2
Joseph Clark	30	30
MASON COUNTY		
William Curley	2	2
Thomas Kilgore	4	4
MECKLENBURG COUNTY		
Robert Jones Qut	35	35
Patrick Hamilton	15	15
Francis Hicks	3	3
Robert D. Wilson qut	11	11
Alexander Field	102	102
MIDDLESEX COUNTY		
Thomas F. Spencer	9	9
Almond Atkinson	1	1
Carter Braxton	1	1
Jane Crittenden	1	1
William Jessee	1	1
MONROE COUNTY		
Town of Union		
Alexander & Co.	3	3
MONTGOMERY COUNTY		
Thomas Helms	3	3
MORGAN COUNTY		
Cunrad Claycomb	8	8
Joseph Kenny	5	5
NANSEMOND COUNTY		
Mills Riddicks quarter	76	78
T. Smelley's quarter	3	3
William S. Riddicks (quarter)	25	25
Jacob Keelings (quarter)	58	58
Abram Brinkleys (quarter)	3	3
Dempsey Jones (quarter)	12	13
Ro. B. Young's Quarter	15	16
Abram Riddicks (quarter)	8	9
NELSON COUNTY		
John Farrar	12	12
John Horsley	36	36
Richard Stevens	6	6
Est. John M. Shelton	12	12
NEW KENT COUNTY		
Jno. M. Delcampo (by Ro. M. Crump his overseer)	15	15
Francis Jordan (by Edw. Watkins)	83	88
Hopewell Parsons' est. (by W^{m}. Lockel, overseer)	9	10
Lewis Smith (by Zach. Shackeford, overseer)	14	15
Conrad Webb (overseer)	96	100
NORTHUMBERLAND COUNTY		
Jno. Bailey	7	7
William Forrester	2	2
Mary Gordon	4	4
Mary Kirkham	8	8
James Bell	4	4
Shepherdstown		
Catharine Devonshire	3	3
Nancy Swearengen	1	1
Limer Swearengen	2	2
Charles Town		
William Robinson	5	5
Wm. & Jas. Kelly	17	17
Robert Latham	4	4
Thos. H. Lansdell	2	2
Benjamin Lamkin	1	1
Samuel Leland	2	2
John Middleton	21	21
Richard Payne	4	4
William D. Robinson	16	16
John S. Tapscott	1	1
Ann Thompson	9	9
NOTTOWAY COUNTY		
Est. Robt. Dickerson	16	16
James H. Fitzgerald	70	70
John H. Dupuy	9	9
Est. Peter Jones	7	7
Sarah Robertson	14	14
John T. Lee	14	14
David G. Williams	25	25
Est. William Daswell	16	16
ORANGE COUNTY		
William Porter	11	11
Benjaman Porter	23	23
PATRICK COUNTY		
Arch^{s}. Hylton (non-resident)	3	3
PITTSYLVANIA COUNTY		
P. Harston's Plantation	16	16
Abram Lydnor Decd	40	40
Thos. Stamps (H. F.)	15	15
Robt. Lewis' Estate	3	3
POWHATAN COUNTY		
Joseph Jenkins	6	6
Edwd. Cox	23	23
William Eggleston	1	1
Edwd. C. Mosby	5	5
Est. Saml. Swann	3	3

VIRGINIA—*Continued*

Name	Slaves	Total	Name	Slaves	Total
PRINCE EDWARD COUNTY			Thomas.................	3	3
Nathl. E. Venable & Co......	20	20			
Philip Watkins, estate.......	27	27	ROCKINGHAM COUNTY		
Ditto as Guardian for Mary			Daniel Utz...............	8	8
R. Watson..............	5	5			
Thomas L. Jones (Buck-			SHENANDOAH COUNTY		
ingham.................	2	2	*Woodstock*		
Collin Stokes (Lunenburg)...	29	29	Suckey Kitchen...........	2	2
William Doswells estate.....	8	8			
Josiah LeGrand estate......	7	7	*1st Batts. of 13 & 97 Regmts.*		
Simon Wooldridge estate....	7	7	*Shenandoah*		
Joel W. Flood (Buckingham)	14	14	Polly Allen...............	3	3
Daniel Bagby (Buckingham).	5	5	Moses Buck...............	2	2
John Morriss (Buckingham).	9	9	Henry Hopewell...........	6	6
Thomas Archer Fowlkes					
(Lunenburg).............	17	18	*2nd B 13 Rt.*		
Henry Brazeal (Amelia).....	17	18	John Beale...............	4	4
PRINCE GEORGE COUNTY			SOUTHAMPTON COUNTY		
Erasmas Roper...........	2	2	Blows Mill...............	8	8
James B. Kendall.........	8	8	Nancy Miller.............	19	19
Thomas Lee..............	5	5			
Robert Gilliam Jr..........	7	7	SPOTSYLVANIA COUNTY		
			John Cobler (estate)........	9	9
Petersburg			Fielding Lucas (estate).....	12	13
John V. Wilcox...........	23	23	Thos. Proctor (estate)......	5	5
Alden B. Spooner..........	5	5	Sup't at Mr. E. Taylor's farm	34	34
Thomas D. Watson........	3	3	William Storke...........	6	6
Elizabeth Taylor..........	1	1	James H. Fitzgerald (estate).	9	9
Robert Birchett...........	3	3			
George A. Spiller's (slaves)..	13	13	*Fredericksburg*		
James Croyton's (slaves)....	22	22	Cornelius Law.............	2	2
PRINCESS ANNE COUNTY			STAFFORD COUNTY		
James M. Whitehurst.......	8	8	George H. Tolson..........	4	4
Henry Wells..............	9	9			
James Henley.............	4	4	*Landoner (?)*		
James Nimmo.............	4	4	William B. Tyler...........	13	13
Daniel Stone..............	5	5	Sarah Beale..............	3	3
Jno. N. Walke............	7	7	John H. Wallace...........	4	4
Eliz. Stone...............	6	6	Frances Daniel............	13	13
Geo. McIntosh............	12	12	Sarah T. Daniel...........	5	5
			Emily Daniel..............	2	2
PRINCE WILLIAM COUNTY			Frances Fitzhugh..........	37	37
Solomon Hill..............	8	8	Gustaˢ. B. Wallace	2	2
			Jamˢ. Rawlins	4	4
RICHMOND COUNTY			Will Beverley.............	22	22
Hannah Smith............	6	6	John T. Lomax............	14	14
William Saunders (Non Res.)	1	1	Rawl: W. Downman........	25	25
William Henderson (Non			John Stone...............	6	6
Res.)...................	11	11	Amy Eddrington...........	5	5
Overseer of Gen'l J. B. Harvie	33	35	Elija Hansborough	6	6
			Steven French.............	22	22
ROCKBRIDGE COUNTY			Willi P. Bailey.............	5	5
Burton's Farm............	26	26	Willi: Ford	5	5
Samuel Cunningham........	5	5			
Mayburg's Forge...........	24	24	SURRY COUNTY		
Prince...................	2	2	Est. B. C. Harrison........	2	2

VIRGINIA—*Continued*

Name	Slaves	Total	Name	Slaves	Total
SUSSEX COUNTY			John Gray Quarter.........	29	29
Harwell's Quarter..........	4	4	Charles Higden Quarter.....	7	7
J. H. Thompson (Gilliam's			Phillip Lightfoot Quarter....	34	34
quarters)	29	30	Harriet Picks Quarter.......	13	13
			Henry Summervill Quarter..	16	17
WARWICK COUNTY			George Turner Quarter......	27	27
William Wynne............	6	6			
			YORK COUNTY		
WESTMORELAND COUNTY			James Semple Senr.........	34	34
Bernard H. Buckner Quarter.	18	18	William Waller............	59	59
William Bernard Quarter....	21	21	William Smart.............	2	2
Fleet Cox.................	5	5